PRAISE I
THE EMPATH E>

"Sydney Campos expertly describes and embodies the experience of living life as a fully empowered empath. When it comes to this topic, there couldn't be a better person to learn from than Sydney. Her personal story shines through as a deeply healing, transformative journey into the depths of darkness that guided her to the light of living from her soul and intuition. Sydney empowers you to shine the light on your shadow to live your most powerful, joyous life. Her story, which is really a guidebook in mastery, not only contains practical tools to support you in living a beautiful life but will also awaken so many souls to living their truth and expressing their unique gifts."

—PRESTON SMILES, author of *Love Louder: 33 Ways to Amplify Your Life*, cofounder of The Bridge Method, and international thought leader

"*The Empath Experience* is a powerful book that will help you awaken your intuitive superpowers while living a life beyond your wildest dreams. Sydney Campos's comprehensive guide and transformative wisdom will inspire you to uncover and transmute old conditioning and step into your power."

—KUTE BLACKSON, transformational teacher and author of national bestseller *You. Are. The. One.*

PRAISE FOR
THE EMPATH EXPERIENCE

"*The Empath Experience* is a must-read for anyone awakening to their psychic sensitivity, heightened emotional and energetic awareness, and capacity for intuitive mastery. Sydney's personal story, as well as the comprehensive guidebook entailed throughout, serves as a powerful support with practical tools and applications for living your most empowered, joyful, loving life. Sydney is not only extremely relatable; she expertly shares profoundly activating experience and anecdotes that will surely serve to awaken your soul to your own deepest embodiment of truth."

—ATHERTON DRENTH, author of *The Intuitive Dance*

THE

Empath

EXPERIENCE

WHAT TO DO WHEN
YOU FEEL EVERYTHING

SYDNEY CAMPOS

ADAMS MEDIA

NEW YORK   LONDON   TORONTO   SYDNEY   NEW DELHI

Adams Media
An Imprint of Simon & Schuster, Inc.
57 Littlefield Street
Avon, Massachusetts 02322

First Adams Media trade paperback edition May 2018

ADAMS MEDIA and colophon are trademarks of Simon & Schuster.

For information about special discounts for bulk purchases, please contact Simon & Schuster Special Sales at 1-866-506-1949 or business@simonandschuster.com.

The Simon & Schuster Speakers Bureau can bring authors to your live event. For more information or to book an event contact the Simon & Schuster Speakers Bureau at 1-866-248-3049 or visit our website at www.simonspeakers.com.

Interior design by Katrina Machado

Manufactured in the United States of America

10 9 8 7

Library of Congress Cataloging-in-Publication Data
Campos, Sydney, author.
The empath experience / Sydney Campos.
Avon, Massachusetts: Adams Media, 2018.
Includes bibliographical references and index.
LCCN 2017061354 (print) | LCCN 2018007958 (ebook) | ISBN 9781507207161 (pb) | ISBN 9781507207178 (ebook)
LCSH: Self-actualization (Psychology) | Emotions. | BISAC: SELF-HELP / Personal Growth / General. | BODY, MIND & SPIRIT / Inspiration & Personal Growth.
LCC BF637.S4 (ebook) | LCC BF637.S4 C3436 2018 (print) | DDC 152.4/1--dc23
LC record available at https://lccn.loc.gov/2017061354

ISBN 978-1-5072-0716-1
ISBN 978-1-5072-0717-8 (ebook)

ACKNOWLEDGMENTS

To Mom, Dad, and Silas. I love you. Thank you for teaching me what it means to love and be loved. Thank you for choosing to be here with me for this incredible adventure. I wouldn't have it any other way.

To my cosmic love, Joe, for seeing me through all dimensions, for holding me and maintaining eye contact for longer than we ever thought possible, and for sponsoring my beach house writing retreat to wrap up this baby.

To my worldwide soul fam, my tribe, my cosmic star family, my dream clients, my cocreators, my cheerleaders. I love you. I see you. Thank you for choosing to be here with me on this magical unfolding path. Thank you for your encouragement. For being the most perfect mirrors ever, reminding me of my truth, and continually catalyzing our collective next-level evolution and expansion. The transition team is officially assembled. Watch out, world.

To my soul sisters: Shelly, Dayana, Taylor, Angele, Jennifer, Naomi, and Anayana. Thank you for simply being. I love you beyond words. Thank you for your hearts.

To John, for always listening and reading my insanely long downloads here and there. I love you.

To James, for showing me the way when I was first learning to see.

To Rebecca, for being my first coach, my first healer, and the first activator of my empathic awakening. Thank you for everything you share, and thank you for choosing to be here and loving the way you do.

To Mama Bali, for your sweet magic medicine.

To my mentors, advisers, and teachers across all dimensions, time, and space. Thank you for triggering me, for activating me, for your constant invitations to rise into even more powerful expression, and for reminding me again and again of why I came here.

To my fantastic team at Simon & Schuster, Eileen and Laura—thank you INFINITELY for your beautiful insights and wisdom shared throughout this epic process: what a dream team indeed! I am so grateful for you. Let's do this again.

CONTENTS

FOREWORD

To the kid who was too scared to speak up in class because the energy emanating from around the classroom was too overwhelming. You didn't quite understand what was happening at the time so you just kept quiet, silently beating yourself up because you couldn't speak up. You knew the answer, but feeling that everyone around you was judging you made it too intense for you to actually voice it.

To the parents of highly intuitive, empathic children who feel powerless or disconnected because they don't understand how to interact with such a sensitive child who feels everything so strongly.

To those who have always felt so deeply the pain of the collective: the oppression, historical separation, and exclusion plaguing humanity for eons. You've always known deep down that those characteristics should not define our collective human experience. You've always known that we're meant to follow a more loving, connected, beautiful way.

To the sensitive souls who've always felt like you're not from this planet: you are here for a reason.

You're here to help create life as we are meant to experience it—heaven on earth at last.

You're here to help us all remember who we are and why we came here.

You are the awakeners.

You are the soul seers.

You are the light bearers.

You are the visionaries.

Your work is simply this: commit unrelentingly to being as authentically YOU as you could ever possibly be.

Always seek, speak, and embody YOUR truth and nothing less.

Never quit when your ego or anyone outside of you says it's time to give up.

Always lean into trust and faith in YOU and know that you're here for greatness, nothing less.

Trust your desires and follow your joy. What lights you up is not random.

Ask for help when you need to leap.

You're never alone, even when you feel like it. Your soul family is all around you.

Are you allowing yourself to be seen and heard?

Not everyone will understand where you're coming from.

Some people in your life will get left behind. Or at least it might feel like that.

Know that you're not leaving anyone behind; you're just evolving in synchronicity with the divine.

Some will be confused.

Remember, it's not your responsibility to be understood.

You are here to raise questions and explore curiosities, creating the new ways of being we all seek to experience.

Some people will feel like you're abandoning them.

But what's not meant for you will naturally fall away when you truly shine at your brightest capacity.

Those who aren't meant to yet understand will find their way in their own time.

It's not up to you to save anyone.

In fact, no one needs saving.

You are a true perfectionist in every sense of the word.

You know that everything is perfect as it is. You can see the gift in every moment.

Your deep capacity to feel is a miracle, activating within you so many powerful capabilities.

Your journey into embodying the fully empowered being that you are will lead you to become the most authentic, loving, powerful version of you that you can possibly be.

Don't you see how precious you are?

There's no one else like you.

And all the while you've learned to look like, be like, act like, and feel like someone else—to fit in.

To be loved.

To be smart.

To be cool.

To be enough.

To feel safe.

You know you are at your core all of these things and so much more.

There are no words to describe your beauty.

Your infinite power.

Your visionary soul.

Your superpowered empathic intuitive gifts.

Your pure love.

You are pure love.

I see you.

Syd

INTRODUCTION

The empath experience is most certainly a unique one. It can be challenging, and at times heartbreaking, to feel absolutely everything at such a deep level, but the same depth of feeling is also glorious, empowering, and filled with expansive possibility. If you identify as an empathic soul, welcome to a beautiful multidimensional existence ripe with infinite opportunities for growth, fulfilling service, and heart-centered leadership.

How do you know if you are an empath? Do you find that being in a public place can be totally overwhelming? Do your friends and family members constantly unload their problems on you, looking for advice on what to do? Do you find that you connect so closely with other people's experiences that you actually *feel* their emotions? Have you ever entered a group setting and immediately felt a deep resonance with the collective energy of the space, almost as though you've absorbed the dominant emotions contained within the group as your own?

Chances are, you picked up this book because you identify with the reality of feeling absolutely everything. You know what it's like to feel other people's pain, worry, fear, sadness, elation—you name it—as your own. You also know what it's like to have been born wanting to be of service, wanting to help save the world, wanting to help other people feel peace and happiness. You know at a deep level that you're here for something that is greater than you—that you are meant to contribute positively to humanity in a special way that only you can. But up until this moment you haven't been able to hear what your specific directive is. You know it's there somewhere; it has to be. You wouldn't have such a strong intuition and emotional sensitivity if that weren't the case. You have such incredible superpowers, but you're not sure how to use them, and more than that, you're not sure if you can trust yourself yet to fully share. You've learned over the years to protect yourself. After all, feeling everything going on around you at all times is overwhelming. Perhaps when you were younger it even felt scary, sad, confusing, or painful. Without a word to describe what you were feeling, perhaps you felt like something was wrong with you—or that you were alone without anyone to genuinely understand what it felt like to be you.

All of this indicates that you are likely awakening to your empathic sensitivity, recognizing that you have the ability to feel the emotions and energy of other people. Being a highly sensitive person may seem like a burden at times, but it certainly doesn't have to be. Being an empath is actually a beautiful gift that you can use to your advantage in a multitude of creative, empowering ways, many of which you'll be guided through over the course of the following pages.

I can identify with all of these experiences because I'm an empath myself. But when I was younger, I had never heard that term and had no idea how to simply exist within my everyday life. To cope, I learned to shut off my intuition and mute my heightened emotional sensitivity. It's actually hard for me to remember parts of my childhood and adolescence because I was so disconnected from myself and so out of touch with my actual internal experience and true perspective. At a certain point in my life I began to take direction from everyone else's emotional experiences and expectations as opposed to sourcing guidance from within myself. I learned to master the art of being who and what I suspected others wanted me to be so I could please them. I believed that if I looked good, if I made others laugh, if I made others feel good, and if I seemed smart and special, people would love me.

Only in hindsight am I conscious of what was going on back then. I was simply doing whatever I perceived was needed at the time to feel safe, to feel like I fit in, and to feel loved. That's all I ever wanted, and that's all most people ever want. I always wanted to feel like I was a part of whatever group or unit I came into contact with. I wanted to feel connected. At a deeper level that I now identify as my soul, I always felt an intense loneliness. And even before I was able to speak, I sensed that something was off—that something wasn't right about this new place I found myself in. Why was there so much fear and stress in the air? I could feel it all before I even understood what was going on around me. Before I understood worldly structures, society, culture, and the rules of interaction, I sensed within my own being an overflowing reflection of the surrounding repression, separation, and suffering. And so I learned to start protecting myself as best I could.

To be authentic means to be true to oneself. It is a very, very dangerous phenomenon; rare people can do that. But whenever people do it, they achieve such beauty, such grace, such contentment that you cannot imagine.

—Osho

The truth is, even if it hasn't felt like it at times (or maybe ever), you hold the power within you now to create a happy, loving, and abundant life. You always have. You have everything you need. What's more, your heightened emotional awareness is actually a gift. These have been the biggest lessons on my path from confusion and disconnection to radical truth and infinite love.

My ongoing journey continues to amaze me with its boundless gifts, expansion, and opportunities to be of service to others in the most fulfilling, nourishing ways—largely due to my deeply alchemical work in the realms of self-love, self-worth, forgiveness, and empowerment. It's my pleasure to present this book as a culmination of the accessible practices, tools, and insights that have empowered me to enjoy a deeper, more authentic, inspired life than I ever could have imagined. My journey is always unfolding, and as you'll see throughout the following pages, living an empowered life is about enjoying the journey while freeing yourself from any attachment to the end destination. Prepare to experience life far more abundantly, lovingly, creatively, and expansively than ever before. *The Empath Experience* will teach you how to understand the emotional connections you feel and how to embrace them in a way that serves you. You'll stop fearing and muting your heightened emotional awareness and start loving who you are and enjoying the world within and around you.

No matter what your experience has been thus far, you're reading this message for a reason. You're meant to be here, right now, in this perfect moment. Talk about divine timing. You are ready to step into a new level of clarity and empowerment beyond anything you've ever experienced. You are ready to take back your power that you've given away (albeit subconsciously) to so many outside circumstances, situations, and people up until this moment. *The Empath Experience* will guide you on your journey.

There's never been a more perfect moment to be fully empowered to step into your individual strengths and abilities, especially when it comes to your intuition, empathy, creativity, and connection. Let's rise, together.

HOW TO USE THIS BOOK

Imagine this book as your map to navigating the many facets of your authentically optimized multidimensional self. Throughout our journey together you will:

- Acquire tools and techniques to strengthen your intuition and develop a deeper clarity around your sensory perception.
- Master your intuitive superpowers, which are innately intended to help you feel supported, connected, and purposeful in your bold, beautiful life.
- Gather lessons from the anecdotes of other empaths and interactive exercises in this book to help you rediscover your hidden genius, your unique gifts, your true passion and purpose, and elements of your being that you might have forgotten.
- Learn to trust your own innate wisdom, follow your own customized internal GPS, and start living a truly fulfilling life completely aligned with your purpose.
- Remove and release any blocks in your way to experiencing life as you truly desire living it with the utmost trust, confidence, and clarity.

You are a courageous soul who's heard the call (and maybe even received some signs from the universe) that it's definitely time for a change. There's an urgency instilled in you to start doing things differently. The old way simply won't cut it any longer. You are the leader of your own life, and it's time to start acting like it. Forget about *acting* like you have it all together. That won't work any longer. It is time to go for full-on embodiment, to live your life as you were meant to live it.

Sounds like a tall order? It might sound like one at first, but you're literally designed to rise to the occasion. The timing has never been more perfect. You are so ready.

To allow this book to support you to the fullest capacity, consider the following guidelines:

IDENTIFY INSTEAD OF COMPARE. All the experiences shared in this book (by me and other empaths like us) are simply meant to provide an opportunity for you to derive your own answers, your own innate truth, and your own custom-tailored guidance. You get to be your own guide, your own best teacher, your own guru. Whenever the inkling to compare yourself to someone else pops up, take back your power by asking yourself how you can give yourself what you need in this moment.

TAKE WHAT YOU NEED AND LEAVE THE REST. If something in the book doesn't resonate with you, turns you off, triggers you, or makes you uncomfortable, become a conscious but nonjudgmental observer of your reaction as much as possible. How is this trigger a gift? How is there a perfect lesson to be learned in your supposed discomfort? How is this trigger a growth experience supporting you in moving into your next level of emotional intelligence and maturity? Conversely, if you find portions that resonate with you, consider how you can best integrate them with your own unique insights and experiences and apply them to your life moving forward. Do you find it helpful to take notes in a journal, highlight portions in the book, make annotations in the margins, or record voice memos of stand-out tidbits? Do what feels best to you, but commit now to fully engage with this text, because it's meant to be studied, engaged with, and reflected on again and again. That's what embodiment is all about—living it and truly BEING it.

3. BE CONFIDENT. This book is for everyone, truly—irrespective of your "level" of meditation, spirituality, self-care, emotional intelligence, or intuitive insight. All human beings have the capacity to tune into their innate empathic nature; however, not everyone is awakened to their energetic sensitivity. Regardless of where you are on your awakening journey, you will find something of value to support your growth and evolution in the following pages, I promise. At this point, ask yourself what it is you intend to learn. What information and support would you find most beneficial right now? What kinds of tools will help you the most given where you are on your path? What is it you are seeking to master and lean into? I suggest doing a brief meditative and journaling reflection with the aforementioned questions in mind before diving in (see the Where Are You Now? exercise in Chapter 1 for instructions). Always keep in mind how powerful it truly is to set your intentions beforehand. You will have a much more grounded, present, and fruitful engagement with this material as a result.

4. TAKE CARE OF YOURSELF. Throughout this book you'll be offered tangible practices and tools to put into action—some of which will initially feel energetically taxing, especially as you get used to using your discernment and energetic focus in new ways. It's like going to the gym for the first time to work on new muscles: expect to feel a bit exhausted at first (followed by a powerful new burst of energy at finding out how much time, focus, and clarity you'll create once you put these practices into full motion). You'll learn quickly through this process that the most important thing you can do for yourself as an empath is take care of yourself and remember that you truly are the most important person in your life. What does top-notch self-care mean for you? How do you give yourself what you need? This book will guide you in creating a sustainable self-care routine

that will be your foundation for empowering your intuitive gifts throughout your daily life and beyond.

5. MAKE A LIST OF ALL THE THINGS IN YOUR LIFE THAT FEEL DRAINING. These could include relationships, obligations, projects, or situations that drain your energy. Then ask yourself how you can release these things that are draining you. How can you drop obligations that aren't fulfilling? How can you end relationships that aren't nourishing you in the ways you deserve? How can you take more time to focus on whatever it is that truly nurtures your mind, body, and soul in the ways you truly desire? You'll find more guidance on this form of energy clearing throughout the book, but it's never too late to get a head start so you're even more prepared for what's to come.

Get ready to emerge from the intuitive, spiritual, psychic-sensitive shadows and courageously face anything that is stopping you from truly utilizing your unique gifts to their fullest capacity.

You know you deserve it.

And you know that it's part of your destiny to start sharing exactly what you have to offer.

The world is waiting to receive you.

CHAPTER 1
Empaths 101

I first learned the word *empath* when I was about twenty-five years old. Perhaps I had heard it before—I'm not sure I remember exactly—but in any case, it didn't fully land until I was truly ready to receive it. You see, it had taken me a long road of searching and some suffering to get to the place where I was truly ready to start taking care of myself.

I followed a pattern of codependency in my relationships starting in middle school well past college. I couldn't be alone, and I focused all my energy on my relationships—like it was my purpose in life to be attached, but also to make sure my partner thought highly of me. Subconsciously I was operating under the belief that if my partner loved me enough, I could fill the void within me that was desperately seeking validation and love.

I also spent nearly a decade abusing drugs and alcohol, with a predominant love for alcohol. Alcohol, you see, helped me feel like I could breathe. My entire life, particularly from middle school and into high school, I really couldn't breathe all the way, especially whenever I was around other people. It felt so overwhelming. I would turn red and freeze whenever the attention was directed to me to speak in front of a group, which would kick into gear a chain reaction of the most painful nervousness and deep-set anxiety imaginable. At the start of high school, I discovered that alcohol helped me shut down my emotional overload and calm my intensely active mind, which was constantly dissecting everything going on around me. Being drunk felt like taking a much-needed vacation from carrying the weight of the world on my shoulders.

Ultimately it was my confusion at processing such a high degree of energetic stimulation as an unidentified empath for so much of my life that sent me into a downward spiral of self-medicating in order to avoid experiencing what to me were far too overwhelming feelings. After getting sober, just after my twenty-fourth birthday, a few friends suggested I try out a Reiki treatment to help me feel more balanced and connected to my own energy. (Reiki is a gentle meditative energy healing technique with roots in Japan that works via an attuned therapist to channel and balance energy throughout your body and clear emotional and energetic blockages, and expedite the body's own innate natural ability to heal.) I was desperately seeking to feel more at peace, so I was willing to try anything.

I first heard the term *empath* right after my first Reiki treatment when I was coming out of a deeply relaxed state. My Reiki healer actually likened me to an emotional sponge, explaining that the reason I had felt so weighed down was because I had been absorbing energies and emotions from other people and even from certain environments. I had been doing this all subconsciously for a long time, quite possibly for my entire life. Everything I was hearing made so much sense. Finally I had a word to describe how I had felt my whole life—*empath*. At that moment I sensed the opening of an intensive new chapter in my own personal development and evolution. There was no turning back.

Even considering all the dark times along the way, I am so grateful for every experience along my path, because each one has prepared me to be of service in unique ways. In sharing my story, with all its darkness as well as its ever-expanding light, it's my sincere hope that you will identify with the underlying feelings and emotional experiences I describe while also being awakened to the many other avenues to empowerment and healing that exist outside of escaping your present reality by self-medicating or other means. One of the biggest gifts I've received along my path is the genuine joy and pure celebration of tuning into this perfect present moment—the space of infinite possibility and true genuine connection in which we meet, at last.

WHAT IS AN EMPATH?

An empath is someone born with the innate ability to feel and understand what other people (as well as other living things such as animals and in some cases even plants) are feeling and experiencing. The key to deciding whether or not you are an empath is to ask yourself if you truly feel the energetic, emotional, and physical experiences of other living beings, or even the entire planet, as though they were your own.

Being an empath is also often associated with clairsentience, which signifies an intuitive ability to intentionally harness empathic tendencies as the gifts that they truly are. That's right, being an empath comes with special superpowers, especially once the gift bearer becomes consciously aware of his or her unique capacity to feel and process energetic information at such a heightened degree.

BEING AN EMPATH VS. BEING EMPATHETIC

The empath experience is not to be confused with feelings of compassion or empathy. Every living being is to some extent empathic, but certain beings experience the condition more strongly than others and as such may identify as empaths outright. If you feel compassion or empathy toward others, you may feel sadness, hopefulness, or perhaps a desire to help them feel better. If you are an empath, you will experience the pain, suffering, emotions, and/or physical sensations or other emotional, spiritual, or physical information emanating from other beings as though it is your own. You may also feel hopefulness or a desire to help other beings.

Let's say a friend tells you that his longtime family dog passed away recently. A person experiencing empathy would feel sad for the friend, have compassion for the effect this loss has had on everyone connected to the dog, and would perhaps offer to help in some way before moving on with his day-to-day life. An empath, however, wouldn't only feel empathy and compassion for the loss, but would also feel the depth of sadness, loss, possible depression, and grief as though this loss had happened to her personally. If the friend describing the loss of the family pet is feeling a heaviness in any particular part of his body—perhaps pain in his stomach and a headache from not sleeping very well—the empath is likely to feel these same bodily aches in her body as well, just like they were her own.

And instead of feeling compassion and then simply letting it go, the empath would continue to be affected emotionally and physically for days or possibly even longer depending on how intensely the experience has been imprinted.

As an empath, sometimes it can even feel like you're reading other people's minds, like you can thoroughly understand what another person means in the deepest sense of whatever it is he or she is trying to convey. And all of this happens subconsciously, without even trying. It's your automatic program, always running on high alert.

HIGHLY SENSITIVE PERSONS (HSPs)

Another interesting consideration when it comes to empaths and other intuitive distinctions is the difference between empaths and highly sensitive persons (HSPs). Elaine Aron, PhD, from the Foundation for the Study of Highly Sensitive Persons, estimates that 15–20 percent of the world's population is highly sensitive. No one knows exactly how many HSPs are also empaths, but it doesn't really matter—what's important is that you know you're not alone as an empath. The thing that sets HSPs apart is their extremely sensitive nervous system. They tend to be affected more by temperature, sounds, and visual stimulation than non-HSPs.

TYPES OF EMPATHS

There are as many types of intuitive beings as there are people on the planet, since every individual operates from a unique perspective.

EXERCISE: HOW DO YOU KNOW IF YOU'RE AN EMPATH?

Use this checklist of common indicators to see how you self-identify:

- **YOU FEEL OTHER PEOPLE'S PAIN.** Physical, emotional, spiritual—you name it. When other people are feeling down, you automatically sense their feelings and even subconsciously take on that pain as your own. You can't help it. You've always wanted to help other people and take care of them; it's part of the natural fabric of your being. It's who you are.
- **YOU CAN READ THE ENERGY—OR "VIBE"—OF A ROOM SOMETIMES EVEN BEFORE ENTERING THE SPACE.** You might also get overwhelmed easily when you're in a crowded situation even for a few moments.
- **YOU HAVE A POWERFUL EMOTIONAL RESPONSE (EVEN TO THE DEGREE OF MAKING YOU FEEL ENORMOUSLY UNCOMFORTABLE) TO TV, MOVIES, OR THEATRICAL PERFORMANCES.** You may have even felt the desire to stop watching or engaging in whatever it was that you were viewing because the experience was too painful, almost as though it were really happening to you.
- **YOU HAVE TAKEN ON OTHER PEOPLE'S ILLNESSES OR PHYSICAL MALADIES.** These could include a cold, allergies, a cough, or physical pain or inflammation. Have you ever suddenly started feeling congested simply because someone around you is sick or has allergies?
- **YOU EXPERIENCE INTENSE EXHAUSTION, ESPECIALLY AFTER SPENDING TIME WITH AN INDIVIDUAL OR A GROUP THAT FEELS IMMENSELY DRAINING ON YOUR ENERGY.** It can feel at times as though you attract certain people because you make them feel better just by your presence, and this interaction often leaves you drained, like you've given so much of yourself without receiving anything in return.

- **YOU FEEL THE COLLECTIVE PAIN AND DIS-EASE OCCURRING THROUGHOUT THE ENTIRE PLANET.** You resonate with the experience of carrying the weight of the world on your shoulders. You are highly attuned to the emotional consequences of violence, oppression, and separation on the global level. You feel responsible for saving the world as a result, because you can see how it might all be able to be fixed.
- **YOU KNOW WHEN OTHER PEOPLE ARE LYING.** You can't explain it, but you've simply always known. You can sense the energetic dissonance of others when they are embodying any type of dishonesty or lack of integrity. As such, you've had challenges with trusting people to the degree that you deeply desire. You're acutely aware of how often people are dishonest, especially with themselves, and you can actually see and feel it. The challenge for you is to be able to not take it personally and consider that you may see something that the other person isn't even yet aware of.
- **YOU ARE SENSITIVE TO NOISE AND LIGHT.** Loud sirens, city noises, traffic, bright lights, and anything that carries with it a feeling of chaos, intensity, or possible confrontation puts you on high alert and can even feel extraordinarily startling. You may feel an aversion to city living, especially if you find yourself surrounded by huge buildings and concrete without easy access to nature or greenery.
- **YOU FIND YOURSELF FEELING INCREDIBLY HEALED AND RESTORED BY NATURE, MORE SO THAN ANYONE ELSE YOU KNOW.** For you, nature is like medicine. You crave the space, peace, quiet, and natural sense of ease provided in expansive greenery, forests, beaches, and mountains. Being in nature nourishes you unlike anything else. Your senses are particularly activated in natural environments, where you may have even had the experience of accessing stronger intuition and psychic foresight.

- **YOU MAY HAVE LEARNED AT A YOUNG AGE TO NOT SAY WHAT YOU'RE REALLY FEELING TO AVOID MAKING OTHER PEOPLE UNCOMFORTABLE.** As a child, you learned to hold back on telling the truth because others, especially adults, weren't able to receive the full degree of your honesty. You may have spoken something so true that others around you felt uncomfortable at having the light shined on an issue or question they weren't prepared to face. Even if their discomfort wasn't voiced, simply sensing the uncomfortable response in them might have made you subconsciously learn that it isn't safe for you to speak your full truth.

Empaths exist across a full spectrum of sensitivities and preclusions. There definitely isn't one template to describe this truly unique experience that is felt across the mental, emotional, and spiritual/energetic realms. However, if you identify with most or all of these circumstances, it's highly likely that your empathic gifts are yearning to be identified and activated. You may sense you are ready to learn how to truly harness your abilities to become fully empowered, energized, and clearly expressed. You're ready to get to know yourself (and your unique gifts) more deeply than ever before so you can live an incredible life marked by connection, confidence, and truth.

Trust that the world is so ready for you.

However, we can narrow it down to the five most prevalent types of empaths: emotional, physical, animal, global, and earth. These are just a few distinctions to reflect on when it comes to the various ways your empath gifts may be expressed. Keep in mind your expression may straddle a few of these and perhaps multiple types at once. Remember, there are as many different kinds of intuition and interpretations of that intuition as there are human beings on the planet: no two souls are the same. There is such a beauty in celebrating our diversity and individuality, knowing that as we shine out our unique frequency we powerfully contribute to the harmony and balance of the collective whole. We are such powerful, divine instruments. Let's learn more about the five most common types of empaths.

EMOTIONAL EMPATH

You pick up the emotions of others. For example, being at a big party filled with excitement, stress, and other intense energy will feel overwhelming due to all the energy being transmitted around you. You may find that when you are around someone who is upset or angry, you will feel upset or angry and you may not understand why you feel that way. The emotional empath experience can be very confusing until you are aware of your tendency to absorb other people's emotions and that you can protect your energy and draw strong boundaries accordingly.

PHYSICAL EMPATH

You can feel other people's pain, physical sensations, and symptoms. If you are near someone who has a headache, for example, you may start feeling that you have a headache as well. If you are around a crowd of people in which many beings have signs of physical ailments, you may start feeling particularly overwhelmed and chaotic. You might find it difficult to recognize if you have a physical ailment or if you are simply mirroring someone else's. If you leave the environment in which you were feeling other people's symptoms, your symptoms might dissipate.

ANIMAL EMPATH

You experience the emotions of nearby animals. You may have a stronger connection to a specific type of animal, such as dogs or cats. Being in situations in which animals are held in captivity, such as a zoo or circus, can be difficult, as the animals may exude a stressful energy that will impact your stress levels.

GLOBAL EMPATH

You pick up the emotions of humans on the planet as a whole. You can absorb the stress of global catastrophes and traumas happening on a mass level, such as natural disasters, mass violence, and war. Everyone can tune into this trauma to some degree, but global empaths are particularly stressed by these occurrences, even without knowing about them via the media or news.

EARTH EMPATH

You pick up sensations and feelings derived from the earth's energy. For example, before a natural disaster is about to strike, you may feel symptoms of stress, nervousness, nausea, back pain, or dizziness that eventually pass after the event is over. People who are not earth empaths will likely experience anxiety and stress after the natural disaster occurs, whereas earth empaths feel the stress and physical symptoms beforehand, signaling the oncoming event—sometimes days ahead of it actually happening.

ANTHONY'S EMPATH EXPERIENCE

I always felt a deep connection to the world around me, sensing a particularly strong kinship to the earth, nature, and the universe.

When I was younger, I felt like I rose with the sun, could gaze at the moon for hours, and as I grew up I started to sense that I could tune into other people's feelings rather easily. I also noticed that people close to me (and even strangers at times) would feel comfortable sharing with me on a deep level—trusting me to be a space for them to be truly seen and supported.

I didn't find out I was an empath until I had my first energy healing session, which I was encouraged to explore upon seeing friends who had experienced wonderful results from similar sessions. After my first session, I felt more aware of my body, mind, and spirit connection. My perceived pathways of energy within my being began to clear and I felt lighter, like the years of spiritual baggage that weighed me down were gone.

WAYS EMPATHS COPE BEFORE THEY UNDERSTAND THEIR GIFTS

Before I had a word to describe my entire life, I simply felt overwhelmed. Furthermore, I didn't even know that what I was experiencing was different from anyone else's daily experience of life. How could I know anything else? What I inferred instead was that everyone else seemed to be living life more easily—like they knew what was going on and what to do and how to fit in. It's like they had a manual for living that I never got. There were so many simple things that felt so incomprehensibly difficult for me to wrap my head around. Could someone just give me the answers?

As I struggled to understand the world around me, I unconsciously created a "manual" of my own containing a wide variety of ways I had developed to cope. If I were to write a book to describe the survival mechanisms I developed early on to mitigate my intensely overwhelming emotional, spiritual, and energetic experiences, here are some of the lessons it would have surely included. You might find that your experiences are very similar.

EMPATH COPING MECHANISM #1:
BE WHO (AND HOW) OTHERS WANT YOU TO BE

When you're an empath, you know what other people like, and more importantly, what they don't like—you can tell what puts them in a bad mood. So you learned from an early age (or at some point along your path) not to disrupt the status quo too much. You wouldn't want to cause anyone to be upset, especially if you know precisely what might set them off.

Empaths are gifted chameleons with the power to transform and shape-shift in an instant to better accommodate whatever situation they might find themselves in. Call it a survival mechanism or a superpower, but empaths can read the energy of a group or of another person they find themselves in contact with and mold to whatever circumstances are present. For example, if you sense someone right off the bat is a calmer, quieter personality who doesn't resonate with intense conversation or powerful language, you might dull down your inclination to communicate aggressively if your personality is more assertive. Or, if you find yourself in a group full of assertive, alpha-type personalities, you might intentionally mirror more of the high energy you sense around you and take on more of a leadership role amid the group.

Shape-shifting can even happen with your appearance. If you find yourself amid a group over a prolonged period, you might start to absorb or emulate the fashion your cohorts display. You might even get complimented for showing off a more desirable style than everyone else because you can read into everyone's preferences so precisely.

Since you practically absorb other people's energy and to some extent their emotions, thoughts, and beliefs, you've likely learned from early on that it's been easier to fit in and accommodate whatever your surroundings dictate than stand out or risk being misunderstood, being made fun of, or worse—becoming an outcast. It's possible that you've mastered the art of being a social chameleon, particularly in school situations, in which you likely proved a complete expert at fitting into multiple social circles and across cultures and ethnicities. In fact, it's possible you've felt at times like you didn't have much of an identity of your own because you could get so caught up in molding yourself to whomever you found yourself hanging out with.

Harmony is our natural state of being, and so, when our energies become too stagnant, chaos is thrown into the mix to stimulate what will eventually result in balance and invite flow. The trick is to not let chaos trap or define you...simply allow it to create movement in the vehicle of your life so that you can snap your eyes open and take back control of the wheel. Do not lose yourself in the storm, instead, be the calm in the storm.

—Alaric Hutchinson, *Living Peace*

And this approach probably worked for quite a while. It did for me, anyway. I remember specifically in middle school feeling proud that I was friends with seemingly everyone—and I went to a huge school with hundreds of groups to navigate across a huge spectrum of cultures. At the time I would joke about having an identity crisis because even I could notice how much my fashion, language, and even style of movement would change depending on who I was hanging out with the most. But at the time that was how I knew how to fit in and create my own type of community. At a deeper level, even if I wasn't aware of it at the time, I was creating a semblance of safety and connection, which was all I ever truly wanted.

What I wouldn't learn until much later is that by being a chameleon and managing other's experiences of me from such a young age, I wasn't actually letting anyone get to know the real me. I wasn't allowing myself to be seen in the way I deeply desired and therefore I wasn't actually open to intimacy or connection in the ways I sought—I was essentially keeping the very thing I wanted out of my reach.

EMPATH COPING MECHANISM #2: DON'T SHARE HOW YOU REALLY FEEL; DON'T BE TOO MUCH

Empaths are highly tuned into harmony, balance, and peace and as such have a special gift of identifying when things are out of balance—whether that be in relationships, in group settings, in an entire environment, or even within larger societal structures. Being wired with this fine-tuned awareness fundamentally designed to help facilitate balance and harmony is absolutely a gift, but it becomes challenging to express when others aren't ready to receive the truth. For example, an empath may enter someone's home and immediately sense how a relationship dynamic present within the home could be improved upon—almost as though the empath understands all sides of the situation and can see where one party could better support the other, thereby bringing the entire relationship into a more optimal balance. But just because the empath understands all sides of the situation as well as how to ameliorate any misunderstanding or tension doesn't mean the parties involved are ready to hear such a suggestion.

Be realistic: plan for a miracle.

—Osho

In kindergarten I remember getting in trouble with the teacher for trying to rally all my classmates to listen up and learn how to play the best game ever. I wanted to teach everyone how to have the most fun; couldn't they see? I learned in that moment that it wasn't safe to stand out and be a leader—I was instead labeled as bossy and seen as a threat to my teacher's semblance of control over our class. She didn't even have to say much to me. In that moment, sensing my teacher's discomfort at perceiving me as a threat to her classroom's order, I learned to keep quiet even if I had a sincere urge to share something in the interest of helping everyone have fun and feel happy.

Since I could feel what others were feeling, sometimes I could tell before my parents even said anything to me if they were going to be receptive to hearing me out in the way I wanted. I could tell if they felt like my teacher back in kindergarten, who was motivated mostly by preventing her power from being usurped. It was through experiences like this that I learned that it wasn't safe to speak up, for I might be considered to be "too much." My emotions, when fully expressed, were overwhelming, not just to people I loved (like my parents), but to me as well. It all felt like too much to hold in one body, in one experience, so I learned to turn it down and not go to such extreme lengths to try to communicate my truth, especially when I already knew it wouldn't be received. No one could possibly understand where I was coming from anyway. Underneath it all I wanted to feel connected and loved, of course, but in order to receive anything close to that I couldn't scare people away by being "too much."

EMPATH COPING MECHANISM #3: TURN DOWN (OR, BETTER YET, TURN OFF AND TUNE OUT) YOUR SENSITIVITY

Turning down your sensitivity might be something you're already aware of having done for quite some time. It might be an unconscious program so engrained in you that for quite a while it seemed like you were altogether somewhat emotionally unaware or unavailable. Until you started to wake up. An awakening to empathic sensitivity can be catalyzed by intense spiritual or emotional challenges, intensive transformation, or even by ecstatic experiences that enliven you to how much love you truly are designed to feel. Just like there are as many types of intuition as there are human beings on the planet, there are infinite ways one can awaken to his or her own inherent empathic sensitivity. And just as there are infinite ways of expressing empathic sensitivity and intuition, there are equally infinite ways to tune out and turn off your abilities altogether.

Think of all the ways we have available to us to check out from reality. There are infinite ways to tune out and turn off our emotions, the most common of which (aside from legal and illegal drugs) are food (including sugar in particular), coffee, tobacco, and alcohol (I would call this a drug too), which are all interestingly enough not only legal but supported year after year with huge advertising revenues and mass market promotion. Media consumption, shopping, overexercising, and really anything else you can think of that could be utilized as a way to check out of your present reality also work incredibly well for dulling energetic and emotional sensitivity.

There are so many ways that you can be distracted from being present with your own being, from tuning into your innate wisdom and gifts. But you have an enormous opportunity to have compassion not only for yourself, but also for all other beings on the cusp of awakening and expanding their consciousness. You can unlearn a lifetime of conditioning that has sought to separate you from your inherent power, from your divinity. And remember that awakening to your true nature of intuitive sensitivity, depth, and intense perceptivity doesn't have to be painful or uncomfortable. However, in my case, I certainly learned the hard way through many rude awakenings that shook me up enough that I finally started paying attention and listening to my soul. And I'm so grateful for every lesson, because I now know and deeply understand that it never has to get worse before it gets better, and waking up doesn't require going through the darkness to get to the light.

For me, when it came to social situations, particularly within school and social activities outside of school, I started checking out from experiencing the full intensity of my emotions early on. Some of the ways I checked out, albeit subconsciously at the time, included attaching myself to one friend or a small group around whom I could feel safe and protected by playing chameleon; with an intense focus on homework and studying so I could avoid social interaction completely; by tiring myself out with intensive sports like swimming or running; and eventually, with drama, gossip, and managing chaos caused by weekends full of drinking and partying.

Partying worked extremely well to support me in disconnecting from my intense emotional experience by giving me other things to focus on instead: drama, relationships, disagreements, planning the activities for the weekend ahead before the current weekend was even over—and on and on. I loved the sensation of not having to focus on what I was actually feeling, even if I didn't know it at the time. I was constantly seeking an escape, so the more things I could focus on outside of myself, the better. The more I could turn it all off, even better.

FIONA'S EMPATH EXPERIENCE

Some of my earliest memories involve confusion and anxiety over why I was constantly feeling ill, why I felt such a heaviness about the world around me, and why I always preferred to avoid crowded situations. I didn't know why, but I felt like people around me were seriously out to get me—and not just that, but also like the world at large was putting pressure on me to fix an insurmountable array of issues that I couldn't possibly see an end to. Of course, I couldn't have explained any of this to you at the time because I was completely unaware of all the different iterations my sensitivity took, but in hindsight everything can be boiled down to one simple fact: I felt everything around me and it was all too much, so I preferred to stay out of it as much as possible. I preferred being alone over being with other kids. I preferred playing games in solitude so I could enjoy myself without having to take care of anyone else. I even asked my mom to homeschool me so I could avoid going to school altogether. The classroom was my archenemy when it came to feeling the unrelenting pressure abounding from everyone's conflicting desires, unmet needs, and multilayered anxieties. Some nights I couldn't sleep because the thought of the horrors terrorizing the planet were too much to bear. I couldn't fathom people being in a war on the other side of the globe while I was in my bed wondering what I might have for breakfast the next day. It wasn't fair.

At one point my parents, being the loving, concerned beings that they are, took me in to a therapist who ran some tests with me to uncover what everyone thought might be an anxiety or attention-deficit disorder. What was instead revealed by some miracle was that I am an ultrasensitive empath. This angel therapist saved my life on that day by using her own intuition and empathic sensitivity no less. She recognized what was going on immediately and had the courage to share her insight as best she knew how, which entailed sharing much of her own experience with coming to similar terms in her own life. I felt so relieved that this person understood what it felt like to be me. I had never felt so understood in my life. And for a moment I even felt free.

Even though I was only twelve at the time, my life up until that point suddenly started to make sense. I immediately received tools to support myself in feeling less drained, in becoming more empowered in my perceptivity and intuition, and most of all, to feel like I had a real gift and a purpose with which to use it in my life. I wasn't an anomaly—I had a reason for being here and incredible gifts to offer, which was all I was really after all along.

EMPATH COPING MECHANISM #4: PLAY IT SAFE; IF YOU GET TOO CLOSE, YOU'LL BE DISAPPOINTED

Playing it safe in relationships is all about protecting yourself from getting hurt—whether that be by creating walls to stem off intimacy, by not letting yourself fall all the way in love, by choosing partners and even friends with whom you can have a codependent or purposefully unequal relationship, and possibly even by managing a completely different identity altogether. This is what it meant for me at least—over many years of one long-term relationship to the next. The same behavior was exhibited in my friendships as well. From an early age I realized that I could protect myself from being hurt or abandoned by always ensuring that I maintained the power in the relationship to some degree. If I knew that the other person needed me, relied on me, and expected me to be in his or her life for a particular purpose, I was safe.

For empaths, being truly vulnerable with another being and allowing yourself to feel to your fullest depth the love you are capable of giving and receiving can feel too intense—almost as though you could implode from being so vulnerable. There may also be a fear of allowing yourself to love more deeply than you believe anyone else could ever love you back. And how painful would it be to feel like such an unequal exchange is occurring. Maybe you really are destined to be alone because no one else can feel all the intensity that you are wired to feel. These fears may very well be present for you if you are awakening to your empathic nature and noticing the ways in which protection mechanisms have developed for you to avoid being hurt by friends, family, or partners.

A huge lesson I learned in my early experience with empath survival was to not get too close in relationships. I could sense early on that if I got too close to people I would run the risk of really seeing them more deeply than they perhaps even saw themselves, and I would see all the incongruences in their personality and ultimately I'd be disappointed with what I found. I only understood this was happening in hindsight, of course, long after coming into my own awareness of my empathic tendencies and the limiting beliefs I developed along the way to protect myself as best I could at the time.

You see, I thought I was protecting myself from being disappointed with what I might find in my relationships if I allowed myself to get too close, but really what was happening all along was the contrary. I was afraid that if I allowed myself to get too close to anyone that they'd see the real me and be disappointed with what they found. Because I didn't know myself and had spent most of my life being whoever I sensed others needed me to be in order to feel comfortable, I essentially had no real identity of my own.

Since I was instead dependent on other people, places, and things to define me and my sense of inherent worthiness, it was extraordinarily difficult for me to connect with others in genuine intimacy. I had made up the excuse at the time that if I got too close I'd be disappointed in them because I'd see them so clearly, but really I was feeling that way about myself all along. I was terrified of being found out: what if they saw that I had no idea who I really was and that I was depending on everyone else to fill this seemingly unfillable void within me, constantly seeking reassurance?

The path to embodying true intimacy continues to be the focus of most of my own personal development to this day, underpinning a constant strengthening of trust in myself and self-esteem along the way. I imagine the same is true for other empaths on this journey of self-discovery and mastery too: the principal challenge remains to experience true intimacy, self-love, and self-acceptance with oneself in order to then in turn experience the same with others in genuine partnership and collaboration.

IT'S TIME TO REWRITE THE BOOK

If you resonate with these coping mechanisms and underlying feelings, welcome. This book is for you. But more than anything, this book is simply a resource to help you create your very own manual based on your truth, your own story, and your own extraordinary, empowered life—one that is free of any coping mechanisms and instead overflowing with strategies to completely thrive from the inside out.

This book is a compilation of tools and practices that have supported me in living a truly empowered, extraordinary life, but overlying everything is my ultimate aim to support you in (re)writing your own story. You see, no one else can write your book quite like you. You have the keys, the map, the compass, and the power to unlock everything you truly desire and all that you deserve in living your best life.

You have everything you need already—now it's finally time to start listening.

Only you can take inner freedom away from yourself, or give it to yourself. Nobody else can.

—Michael A. Singer, *The Untethered Soul: The Journey Beyond Yourself*

WHY BEING AN EMPATH IS A GIFT

You are an absolute gift.

Receive that fully. Let it land and go straight to your heart.

And what a gift it is to have a genuine spirit like yours. You've always wanted to help make the world a better place. But perhaps until this moment you're not sure how your deep desire to be of service and in doing so experience great fulfillment is supposed to materialize. You're also not sure about how to wield your fantastic abilities in all the powerful ways you're meant to. Perhaps until this moment you've felt your gifts mostly as a burden. A heaviness. An unbearable weight.

At a certain level, all souls have the capacity to feel empathically and discern what others are experiencing in their mental, emotional, and spiritual existence. But not all souls are embodied to the extent that you, as you're now reading this, most certainly are.

EXERCISE: CLEAR YOUR ENERGY AND INSTANTLY ACCESS INNER PEACE

Feeling absolutely everything and everyone can be completely overwhelming, so much so that perhaps you even find it hard to remember to breathe. I used to feel that way too—in fact, I would stifle my full capacity to breathe because in hindsight, I felt subconsciously that if I breathed in all the way, I would let even more feeling in. My sensitivity was already overwhelming, why make it any more intense? Little did I know that my breath held the keys to the freedom and peace I had been seeking all along; I just had to learn how to utilize its power.

This exercise is one of the most helpful, simple tools for your empath toolbox, and it's especially useful for moments when you feel like you've absorbed negativity or heaviness that you don't want any part of or if you simply want to feel more centered and grounded in your own being. Here's how to do it:

1. Regardless of where you are or what you're in the middle of doing, take three minutes to sit or stand still. Lie down if you're able to. If you're able to get to an outdoor area covered in grass or natural earth, feel free to take this practice outside to strengthen your grounded, centered feeling even more. Place your bare feet on the ground to directly connect to the earth beneath you.
2. Set a timer for at least three minutes so your mind doesn't need to be focused on keeping track of the time.
3. Breathe in and out as deeply as you possibly can.
4. As you breathe, picture roots growing up from the earth's core and passing through your feet, up your legs, and all the way through your body until they exit through the top of your head. Once the roots exit your head, picture the energy making a connection to the sun, sky, spirit, higher self, infinite source—whatever you feel connected to as a higher power. Continue breathing in and out as deeply as you can.

5. On each exhale, feel anything that doesn't serve you—negativity, heaviness, tension, tightness—falling away and being given back to the earth to be recycled as new, fresh energy. Picture the roots that are moving through your body becoming more illuminated with beautiful healing light that naturally cleanses your system of anything that doesn't serve you, creating space for you to access your heart, your soul, and your intuition with effortless ease.

6. To complete this exercise, say out loud or to yourself any powerful affirmations that help you feel even more strongly grounded in your being. Here are some example statements to consider, but feel free to create your own, trusting that whatever feels best for you is absolutely perfect:

- I am free of all foreign energies.
- I am completely open to receiving divine guidance and inspiration.
- I listen to my powerful intuition that guides my every move.
- I am safe. I am protected. I am well.
- I am peaceful. I am powerful. I am free.

The best part of this exercise is that you can do it absolutely anywhere and it only takes a few minutes to instantly feel its powerful effects. In the beginning of your practice, try setting a reminder alert on your phone to do this a few times throughout your day so you eventually get in the habit of doing it by default.

Then next time you're in a particularly challenging situation or find yourself surrounded by intense energy, you'll know what to do to immediately clear yourself and come back to center. Notice how even a small commitment—such as dedicating yourself to this new practice each day—creates immensely powerful shifts throughout your life.

You have elected to take a warrior path indeed. The empathic journey is just like that. It's one of darkness into light, from shadow into full illumination of the truth, so that you rise to be a beacon for not only yourself but in turn for so many others. How exactly is being an empath a gift?

- IT'S YOUR NATURE TO WANT TO HELP AND SUPPORT OTHERS. To be the light when there seems to be an omnipotent darkness. To feel what everyone is feeling and naturally seek to manage the collective energy in such a way that you help everyone feel more comfortable, to simply be.

- YOU KEEP THINGS SIMPLE. You see how simple it can all really be, this life we all share in this moment. You see that the point is really to love and be loved, just like that. You know that's what we are here for; that's been the whole point all along. You know why you are here when you stop and really listen.

- YOU HAVE A SUPERPOWERED INTUITION THAT'S THE MOST POWERFUL GUIDANCE SYSTEM YOU COULD EVER DREAM OF. You are like a supercomputer, programmed with a direct channel dialed into your inner wisdom that comes in clear at all times—ready to deliver the precise message, service, or action you need in the moment.

- YOU ARE A MESSENGER OF THE DIVINE. While it might feel like your grandest task is to decipher how you can best be of service to the planet, your real task to master is YOU. How can you be the most important person in your own life? How can you love YOU more deeply than any love you've ever known? How can you trust that you are worthy of everything you deeply desire and as such, you are worthy of allowing your most beautiful life to simply flow?

- YOU ARE BUILT TO COCREATE WITH THE DIVINE. You are an instrument of empowerment, of peace, connection and healing.

- YOU ARE EMPOWERED BEYOND BELIEF WITH THE MOST INCREDIBLE SENSORY PERCEPTION. You can avail yourself to profound levels of depth in the full spectrum of your emotional, mental, and spiritual experiences. You can relate to people on a soul level, almost immediately at times.

- **YOU'RE THE PERSON PEOPLE ALWAYS CALL AN OLD SOUL, BECAUSE IT SEEMS LIKE YOU'VE KNOWN THEM FOREVER.** In a way you have known them forever because you see right through to their core and you are in fact feeling their experience of life. Your gift is to help others feel seen for who they truly are, sometimes before they can see it for themselves. You're a mirror like that—which is one of your most powerful gifts.

- **YOU ARE GREAT AT CONNECTION.** You have an amazing ability to connect hearts and minds, and help people to feel truly seen and heard.

- **YOU ARE BEYOND UNDERSTANDING.** You help others feel like their experience isn't just theirs alone, and that perhaps it's happening all according to a bigger plan after all. That just maybe, like they suspect, they are in fact guided along the way as long as they keep listening.

- **YOU HAVE TRUE SIGHT.** You see straight through people's masks and immediately know what's truly bubbling up underneath the surface, regardless of what the person's outward stature may be saying. You see the truth and help support others in fully embodying exactly that.

- **YOU HAVE HIGH STANDARDS, RIGHTFULLY SO.** You see what's truly possible for this beautiful world and you know (almost as though you remember from distant times) the full breadth of human potential. You see everyone in their utmost brilliance—you know we are here for greatness. You remind everyone to never stand for anything less. Never settle. You can't help but be a constant reminder even with your sheer presence.

- **YOU ARE A HEALER BY NATURE.** A nurturer. A lover. You are here to share and experience absolute magic, nothing less.

EXERCISE: WHERE ARE YOU NOW?

As we've covered so far, all people are wired with special intuitive gifts and fundamentally empathic sensitivity, but everyone is on a different trajectory when it comes to operating with distinct levels of awareness. In the pages to follow you will learn all about the various elements of empathic gifts including key examples of how to take care of yourself to further activate your innate gifts. You will most likely feel incredibly activated in your own intuitive wisdom and as such will feel like you have a newly empowered outlook on your life and a whole new way to enjoy it.

Before we dive all the way in—and trust me, we're going deep because that's really the only way we know how—take some time to center yourself around your intentions and establish your foundation point from which you will be launching into a whole new experience of life. You can't possibly know how far you've come until you've taken the time to identify where you started. So, let's begin.

1. Get into a meditative position and prepare to set aside however long you feel is needed to get grounded, calm, and focused in your body, with plenty of time to journal your reflections that abound. I would suggest blocking out at least thirty minutes. Remember, it should feel luxurious to give yourself the gift of space to reflect on your true desires and intentions for our wonderful work ahead. You deserve it.

2. After taking some deep breaths and feeling grounded in your body, perhaps tuning into some calming music to further induce a relaxed, clear state, start to bring to mind the following questions for inquiry and conscious reflection:

    •   Do I resonate with anything in particular that's been mentioned so far in this text? If so, what has resonated most deeply?

- Do I identify as an empath? How so?
- What do I hope to gain from the material presented in this text?
- In which areas of my life do I desire to feel more empowered? How so?
- What are my innate gifts? What are my superpowers?
- What challenges, if any, are in my way of fully sharing my gifts with the world?

3. After your inquiry into each of these questions, decide which modality feels best for you to fully anchor into your reflections and decipher where you stand: journal your responses, create a video response, create a piece of art or visual response, record a voice memo, or share them with a friend. The point is to make a marker of where you are now so you can tune back in after you've finished the work entailed in this text—then you can acknowledge yourself for how far you've come.

CHAPTER 2
Unlock Your Empath Superpowers and Live Your Authentic Truth

From my earliest memories I always sensed I had important work to do in this life, and I knew there was a way my gifts desired being expressed, but for so long the prospect of actually rising to the occasion seemed impossible. The gravity of the situation at hand that I wanted to be a part of resolving felt too massive—how would I ever help shift any of it? I was so attuned to the immense degree of suffering going on across the planet—the inequality, poverty, oppression, violence, you name it— since I was a child, but knowing how widespread it all was, almost saturated beyond belief through every corner of society, whatever was someone like me to do about it?

I wish I had known I had superpowers all along—that what I identi-fied at the time as burdens actually turned out to be some of my most unique, powerful gifts: a keen intuition, an ability to empathize above and beyond with others, a deep understanding of the way the world works and the way in which behaviors and beliefs are learned, and so much more. What used to feel so heavy on my shoulders—a feeling of respon-sibility to save the world and everyone in my immediate presence who seemed to be suffering—was actually the gateway to my entire healing journey and subsequent transformation. I couldn't have asked for a more rigorous education to prepare me more perfectly for this moment.

OWNING YOUR GIFTS

That's right, you have superpowers. Have you ever noticed that you have an uncanny ability to help other people feel better, to see the best in them-selves, to feel empowered? You might have also had the experience of walking into a room and truly lighting it up with your loving presence. Other people might regularly compliment you on your laugh—almost as though it's a healing experience for them to listen to. Others have complimented you on your beautiful voice. Maybe you are a natural artist, a musician, a dancer demonstrating such a divine, graceful flow.

Along with those traits, you might also feel the weight of the world, though—as if it's your job to save humanity from itself. Trust that it's not up to you; it actually never has been. There's no world to save. You're off the hook. What a relief! And the beautiful lesson in this truth is that by taking incredible care of yourself, your positive impact on the world is actually strengthened. By being your best you, especially as the complete embodiment of an empowered, empathic soul, trust that you automatically show up in the world as a loving, radiantly positive light that naturally supports others in their path to align with their best selves too.

You have a being unique and individual, incomparable. It has never been before, it will never be again; only you have got it. Celebrate it!

—Osho, *When the Shoe Fits*

You may think that your gift is to help other people feel good and feel like they can be empowered to live their best lives, but the secret is there's actually nothing you have to do to achieve that. You see, simply by just being you, you are a powerful reminder and invitation for others to embody their fullest light and most expansive joy. Simply by being, you are a healing, loving, radiant presence. You are a gift. Such is your nature. And just like that, you are now being invited to consciously seek to unlock the full array of your empath superpowers and shine more brilliantly than you can possibly imagine.

You're about to delve into your very own crash course in supercharging your empathic abilities, amplifying your gifts in the ways that resonate most powerfully for you. This journey is all about feeling your absolute best no matter what, to feel grounded in your being with a deep sense of trust and calm that allows you to listen to your clear-as-day internal guidance that's always showing you the most perfect path. How do you desire showing up in your fullest expression? What is it like to live your ideal life in every moment? How does it feel to be completely empowered as the creator of your experience? You will find out.

Embodying your supercharged, intuitive, balanced state is your natural flow that you tune into effortlessly once you are in the habit of taking incredible care of yourself (which you'll learn more about in the next chapters). It's time to feel your absolute best as often as possible and most importantly, be completely empowered to be the conscious cocreator of your most powerful, beautiful, expansive life.

BRIAN'S EMPATH EXPERIENCE

I struggled with substance abuse and overeating for most of my adolescence and early adulthood as a direct result of trying to mute my intensely overwhelming emotions. I couldn't handle being human; it felt way too overwhelming. How was I supposed to go to school and interact with anyone, let alone do my schoolwork when my body was completely shocked with anxiety from all the energy being processed in my system? Of course, I wasn't aware at the time that this was exactly what was happening—I just thought something was wrong with me and I needed to do whatever I could to turn it off.

No one else seemed to have this kind of problem, so it was better for me to keep it to myself and just do what I needed to do to get by. That was my MO for a long time—perhaps too long, but in the end, it was the perfect lesson for me to awaken to my true gifts and superpowers of being an empath. I am so grateful for the darkness I've been through, especially because I can share about it all from an empowered perspective that I know helps others to avoid feeling the need to go down a similar trajectory.

I am now an example of what it's like to be an empowered leader when it comes to consciousness and awakening. I have found my calling as a spiritual guide and I've never felt more fulfilled in my life, which just keeps getting better every day as I continue following my truth even more powerfully and sharing my divine gifts. My empathic gifts are the foundation for my life now. I've created my life specifically as an expression of my uniqueness. I am a seer. I am a deep listener. I am a teacher. I am an ancient soul here to light the way for other awakening souls here to cocreate a beautiful existence together on this magical land. Because I am empowered in my empathic abilities and no longer suffer anxiety because I know how to take care of myself, I am an expert at holding space for others to heal and transform and expand in beautiful ways.

Most of all, I am so grateful to know that saving the planet is no longer and has never been my responsibility. I get to focus completely on myself and my well-being to live my best possible life—just in being my most powerful, fulfilled, healthy self I naturally inspire everyone else in my life to do and BE the same. I am so grateful for all of my lessons thus far; they have been so perfectly designed for me to grow in precisely the ways I've needed to grow. All along I've been so divinely guided. We all are, always.

THE GIFT OF SOURCING YOUR OWN LOVE

Most empaths I've known and spoken to all share the common challenge of putting themselves first. This was certainly the case for me for much of my life before awakening to my superpowers and starting along the path of radical self-care and authentic expression. Eventually, one of the most powerful gifts you'll realize you possess as an empath is your keen ability to love yourself and then shine that light out as bright as ever to share with the rest of the world.

UNLEARNING DECADES OF PUTTING OTHERS FIRST

Because most empaths spend decades (or seemingly multiple lifetimes) learning coping mechanisms to take care of themselves before they realize their gifts, many of us have spent a lot of time putting other people's needs before our own. Like any ingrained habit, this one will take some time and a consistent commitment to undo once and for all.

When I tuned into some of my first memories, I realized that I learned at a young age to take care of others, starting with my parents. With my mother specifically I can remember learning to make sure she was happy— was there anything I could do to make sure she was pleased? It makes sense that I wanted to please her—after all, I had spent the first nine months of my human existence in her body and then the following early years completely dependent upon her to take care of me and literally ensure my survival.

Your task is not to seek for love, but merely to seek and find all the barriers within yourself that you have built against it.

—Rumi

What I wasn't aware of at the time, however, was that I was already starting to feel her emotions as my own and was crossing all sorts of energetic boundaries in the process, taking on what I perceived to be stress, anxiety, sadness, or anything else that didn't feel aligned with what I considered to be worthwhile states of being. I had learned subconsciously to equate my mother's happiness with my own sense of security. I had witnessed the moments when my mom was sad or unhappy to mean that she wasn't fully available to take care of me in the ways I required—which to me meant that I couldn't expect to receive the attention I was so heavily dependent upon.

I wasn't consciously aware of any of this at the time; I was just doing what I interpreted was required to receive what I most deeply desired: a feeling of love, safety, and security. But as long as I was sourcing this from outside of myself by focusing all my energy on pleasing everyone else around me first so that I could then be worthy of love, it set me up for quite a grand lesson that wouldn't become fully actualized until many years later. You see, the cycle of seeking love outside of myself via people-pleasing was an addiction of sorts—it never quite hit the spot, so I kept coming back for more, thinking that each time I was a bit closer than the last. I was never actually receiving the love I was craving and I never would, until I learned to source it from within myself.

PUTTING YOURSELF FIRST LEADS TO SELF-LOVE

How do you source love from within yourself? Perhaps it feels like a tall order. The many self-care techniques in this book will go a long way toward helping you. The key to enjoying the lasting benefits of all your practices while creating permanent shifts in the ways you respond to life is relentlessly committing to putting yourself first no matter what. What does putting yourself first really mean? If you're completely new to the idea, it's going to first involve a major overhaul of your deeply ingrained values regarding your worthiness, your self-esteem, and your ability to trust yourself.

As an empath, your most important job is to take phenomenal care of yourself, like you're truly the most important person in your life. Treat yourself like you would a best friend, the most important soul you've ever known, your dearest love. Fall in love with you, your very own beloved. Can you imagine? If you're feeling like this is a tough concept to grasp, you're in good company with your fellow empaths.

So how can taking care of yourself in fact lead to you sourcing your own love from within? Well, in my experience, when I really started to take care of myself because I actually desired doing so—not just because it looked good to do so or because it seemed like the right thing to do based on what others were expecting of me—I started to really care about myself on a deep level, more deeply than I could have ever hoped to experience. I started seeing myself. I started seeing how amazing I truly am. I started appreciating my gifts, my essence, my presence, my beauty. I started to fall in love with my own multidimensional being, with my soul. I started to see how magical I truly am, how much I've been through, how strong I am, how courageous I am. I started to enjoy being in a relationship with myself, and similarly started to love taking care of myself as I would someone I loved—almost as I imagine I would do for my own child. In fact I was caring for my own inner child within. I also started to realize that as I put more of my energy into caring for myself, my relationships deepened because I had a heightened capacity for intimacy. Because I saw myself more clearly and loved myself more profoundly, I was able to show up as a more expansive container of depth and love with others. Instead of seeing self-care as a selfish act as I had in the past, I came to know that self-care and self-love is the foundation for me being able to show up in my relationships with the most incredibly loving presence that I am capable of—which is all I truly ever desired experiencing.

When you adopt the viewpoint that there is nothing that exists that is not part of you, that there is no one who exists who is not part of you, that any judgment you make is self-judgment, that any criticism you level is self-criticism, you will wisely extend to yourself an unconditional love that will be the light of the world.

—Harry Palmer

THE GIFT OF KNOWING THAT YOU ARE WORTHY, JUST AS YOU ARE

First things first: you are powerful and worthy simply because you are. There's nothing you need to know, do, make, create, or prove to be powerful or worthy. Allow yourself to fully receive this truth. It's time to dive in and get to know you on a whole new, celebratory level. You are intrinsically valuable—nothing outside of you defines your worth.

Worthiness, in very simple terms, means I have found a way to let the Energy reach me—the Energy that is natural—reach me. Worthiness, or unworthiness, is something that is pronounced upon you by you. You are the only one that can deem yourself worthy or unworthy. You are the only one who can love yourself into a state of allowing, or hate yourself into a state of disallowing. There is not something wrong with you, nor is there something wrong with one who is not loving you. You are all just, in the moment, practicing the art of not allowing, or the art of resisting.

—Abraham-Hicks

If you've spent a lot of time determining your value based on your outside circumstances (such as your job, your looks, your success, your bank account, your friends, ad infinitum) and what other people think of you, it's time to start rewiring your experience so you can enjoy the gift of a deeper sense of fulfillment that's only possible when your unique value is truly sourced from within.

ACKNOWLEDGING SOCIAL CONDITIONING

First and foremost, it's important to recognize how social conditioning has impacted you. As an empath particularly, it's more than likely you've absorbed much of the values and belief systems of the collective consciousness in regard to worth and what constitutes success. The social fabric into which we are born fundamentally relies on intense levels of inequality and separation to exist in order for all of our social, economic, and political systems to function as intended. Inherently this structure is also built upon a mass cultural agreement that worthiness, love, and power are accumulated through externalized actions and appearances.

You learn who you are by unlearning who they taught you to be.

—Nikki Rowe

I learned early on from advertising and commercials that as a woman, minding my appearance was one of the most important things I could focus my energy on. How I looked defined the way people would react to me, and since I could feel what everyone else was feeling all along, it became critical for me to manage those interactions as best I could by always ensuring I looked my best. Worthiness, or rather an inherent lack thereof, tends to be further exaggerated for empaths not only because of our tendency to absorb the conditioning of the collective consciousness but also due to our own ultrasensitive reactions to marketing and advertising messaging. As we all know, the media is constantly inundating us with examples of how we are not enough for one reason or another. Yet if we all felt genuinely worthy and complete, would we have a reason to buy anything? Certainly not to the scale that capitalism demands. Catch my drift?

RECLAIMING YOUR INHERENT SELF-WORTH

So, if you're an ultrasensitive empath, you have a lot to manage when it comes to healing your own self-worth. And why does it matter? Well, let's dial it back to day one. When you were born, you didn't have a concept of unworthiness or not being enough; it was a nonissue. You lived to be completely embodied in your uniqueness and divine intrinsic value—simply because you are. But in your earliest years of life you created and programmed belief systems that went on to distinguish the ways in which you understand the entire world and how you are to best interact with it all. Imagine running these early belief systems and programs inherited from age three as a thirty-year-old adult. Now imagine how many people are living their lives precisely like that, without even knowing they have an option to awaken to an alternative and change their state of being. Herein lies the invitation for true consciousness evolution and awakening. Herein lies the path to liberation.

Until you source a sense of worthiness from within, the outside purchases and materializations of status will never be enough to sustain the void felt inside. No matter how much more you buy, it simply won't make the underlying feeling of not being enough dissipate.

You are not born to follow the society, you are born to inspire it—
you are born to teach it—you are born to build it.
—Abhijit Naskar, *The Bengal Tigress: A Treatise on
Gender Equality*

You may feel temporary relief, but chances of sustaining a lasting impact are slim if you're thinking that this is an outside fix by any means. If we've learned anything by now, living an empowered, happy, fulfilled, extraordinary life requires starting from within first and foremost. It's always been an inside job.

HEALING UNWORTHINESS

An entire book could be written about this subject alone, that's for sure. But for the purposes of our journey together, it's important to mention that all the self-care ideas in this book will help you heal your self-worth and self-esteem. All practices shared throughout this book will support you in developing deeper worthiness and energetic sovereignty, but here are a few guidelines to follow in getting to the root of your unworthiness story:

- Identify your early memories that may have set some of your unconscious worthiness programming into motion. Can you remember the first time or first few times in your life when you didn't get what you needed from a caretaker and possibly interpreted the situation to mean something negative about you?

- Reflect on other ways you may have given your power away in your life—to other people, to relationships, to your job, to societal constructs of how you were taught to be, to other people's expectations of you, to your own fear of what other people thought or anxiety about whether or not you'd be understood and accepted. Get honest with yourself about where you are.

- Come clean about any areas of your life in which you aren't fully living for you or in alignment with what you truly desire. Look at any area in which you are doing things you don't enjoy because you feel at a deeper level like you have no choice, or that you are operating out of survival.

- Regularly check in with yourself and consider integrating into your life a daily practice of meditation, self-reflection, and journaling on the following prompt: what do you truly desire and how can you create space in your life to receive precisely that?

DEALING WITH TRYING TO FIND WORTHINESS IN OVERPERFORMING

Another way that unworthiness can manifest, especially for empaths, is as an addiction to overdoing, overworking, and overperforming. If you are operating with a belief system rooted in not being enough, and you're constantly striving to prove your value based on achievements and accomplishments, you may already be feeling burned out just reading this sentence. I see you. I used to be like you too. One of the problems with overdoing is that it makes for a great escape from simply being—being with yourself and being quiet and still enough to hear your deeper truth emanating from within and guiding you into greater alignment. The busier you are, the easier it is to avoid the truth. The more you feel you are indebted to showing up for everyone else first, and proving your worth through the accumulation of external accolades, the more disconnected you feel from your inherent sense of value that's only really ever sourced from within.

The real difficulty is to overcome how you think about yourself.

—Maya Angelou

What would it be like to stop doing so much, or stop doing completely? What would it feel like to give yourself space to simply be? Even for a few hours? Even for a few days a week. You might hear some powerful truth as to how you can experience more fulfilling alignment and a sense of ease in your life. Are you afraid of being alone? Being busy is also a great distraction from facing the truth about ourselves. But if you are here to live an empowered life, fully activated to your unique gifts and expansively open to sharing yourself with the world in only the ways you can, it's time to stop overperforming and overdoing.

THE POWER OF WORTHINESS

What's on the other side of feeling worthy? Your self-esteem will automatically improve as you start to take better care of yourself and give yourself what you need without depending on anyone else or anything outside of you to save you. You will exhibit more powerful, magnetic creativity that supports you in multiple dimensions of your life: your livelihood, well-being, relationships, and more. As you establish a deeper sense of trust within yourself, which is an inherent result of increasing your self-worth and self-esteem, you will find that your intuition is more active and communicates with you more clearly than ever. You will find yourself emanating a vibrational resonance that attracts more aligned opportunities, relationships, and gifts to you—just to name a few. You will experience life as a truly divine flow, allowing yourself to be guided in the most perfect ways.

THE GIFT OF SERVICE (NOT SERVITUDE)

To live a fully empowered existence completely activated in their gifts, empaths must understand the crucial distinction between *service* and *servitude*. You are here to enjoy a beautiful and abundant life based on you feeling your absolute best so you can be of high *service* to the planet in the ways in which only you can be. If you've learned to take care of others and place everyone else's needs ahead of your own your entire life, then you've likely learned to be in *servitude* to others on multiple levels. And the thing about servitude is that it can manifest quite subtly. Even when you think you are being of service and doing what's most fulfilling for you, you still might be driven by a deeper motivation to be in servitude to others.

WHAT'S THE DIFFERENCE?

How do you know if you are operating in service versus servitude?

EXERCISE: SHARE YOUR GIFTS WITH THE WORLD

How are you authentically sharing what matters most to you? What do you deeply desire to share with the world? What is your truth? Do you have something deep down that you desire to share with a wider audience? Does the world know your worth? Do you have a vision you want to declare more visibly to yourself and in your intimate relationships? How can you speak this desire and vision into being?

Here's a powerful way to share your gifts while owning your unique worthiness and inherent value:

1. Meditate to tune into your higher self, your soul, and your higher guidance system.
2. Now that you've dropped in deeply to your higher consciousness, intuitively tune in and ask yourself the following questions and write down your answers in your journal:

   • What do I have to declare? Is there something burning within me that I want to share?
   • Do I have a vision, an opinion, or a viewpoint that I feel called to speak to?
   • Is there something I want to create that I can powerfully declare into being?
   • Is there anyone that needs to hear my message right now?

   Pick a platform (such as *Facebook*, *Instagram*, a blog, email, or even a relationship—get creative!) in which you can share your vision, a declaration of your worth, something you're creating, and/or something you simply care deeply about that you feel called to vocalize.

   Make a commitment to communicate whatever it is that matters most to you on the platform. Make a date to share, or better yet, do it now. Don't think about it too much; listen to your feelings and intuition about this as you tune in. Some examples to inspire you:

1. Make a *Facebook Live* stream about something you're curious about, something you're passionate about, or something you're learning.
2. Write a blog post, an article, or a social post about something you care about, something you're celebrating about yourself, something you want to create in your life (maybe your goals and your vision).
3. In a select relationship, share your vision for how you want the relationship to be. What do you desire?
4. Share your personal/professional/creative vision with another counterpart (colleague, boss, friend, partner, community) in a whole new way.
5. Make known your special offerings and gifts on a public platform so people know what you're up to. Reintroduce yourself just because you matter and you deserve to be celebrated.
6. Declare what you're creating at the moment and in the future—what are you looking forward to?

There is so much power in your vulnerability and willingness to be seen celebrating your worth. Plus, when you are vulnerable about your truth, the universe conspires in magical, miraculous ways to support you and help you share your gifts with the world. As always, listen to your desires and let them guide you. Continue seizing every opportunity to speak your truth, which has always been (and will always be) your greatest power.

SERVICE	SERVITUDE
Your highest calling; the thing you'd be doing if you were stranded on a desert island with nothing else to do and nowhere else to be.	A heavy energy synonymous with obligation and possibly a feeling of enslavement to an idea, to an expectation, to a person, or institution.
A truly unique expression of your authentic power and soul-inspired gifts; something that only you can share and embody, that no one else has the same access to.	Sharing in a way that feels like giving your power away and therefore not standing in your own authentic truth or aligning to what is only most meaningful to you and only you.
The thing that feels like you are naturally designed to bring forth through your gifts and your unique expression.	Creating or speaking in such a way that's totally guided by what others think of you, what others want, or what others need.
The thing that's most fulfilling and nourishing for you to share on the soul level.	Feeling motivated to create, share, speak, or show up in a way that is completely dependent on external validation or approval.
Your soul's purpose. It's the key to unlocking your divine flow and opening up to receiving infinite synchronicity to support your massive vision.	Feels like you have something to prove or repay in whatever you're offering instead of sharing from your heart. Do you feel like you're repaying a debt of some kind? Who do you feel you owe and why?
You know you're in service when you're losing track of time, you feel energized, the perfect people and opportunities come into your zone in the perfect moments, and you feel in incredible alignment with your vision for your life. This is what you were built for.	You feel drained energetically, like there's not enough time. You feel stressed out and overall like you're swimming upstream with whatever it is you're creating; nothing is flowing easily, everything feels hard, and no pieces fit together easily.

Servitude is a common trap that empaths especially can fall into if your programming is deeply rooted in urging you to constantly take care of others, accommodate others, and make sure that you're not being too disruptive. You wouldn't want to rock the boat too much. God forbid you make someone else uncomfortable, because of course you would feel completely as though the discomfort was your own.

This dynamic is especially important to differentiate if you are a visionary, a leader, an entrepreneur, an artist, or someone who feels a strong calling to break apart from the mold and create something new that quite possibly doesn't even exist yet. Most empaths are just that—visionary leaders here to genuinely bring new ideas and innovations into being in new ways that haven't ever appeared in the collective consciousness. If you are in service, you will experience more of an easeful flow and receptivity to the unique creativity available to you. If you are in servitude to what you think others think of you, or how you think you might impact and possibly disrupt the collective, you are stagnating your own creative potential and gravely limiting your receptivity of intuitive inspiration to power your efforts forward.

FOCUS ON SERVICE

So what can you do to ensure you are aligned with service as opposed to servitude? Treat yourself like the most important person in your life and only do what you truly love. Follow your highest excitement and joy in all possible ways.

If you're ever settling for less than what you truly desire via practicing servitude, you'll experience a stunted momentum in whatever you're creating as though you're swimming upstream against a powerful resistance. Being in service allows you to effortlessly coast along in the natural stream of life. So as always, follow your best feelings and allow your senses to guide you. Integrate the lessons on offer throughout this text. Make them your own. Support yourself to tune into your inherent worthiness, power, and creative vision that's yearning to come through you. Allow yourself to receive all the divine abundance, love, and fun that you're designed to enjoy. The more you can tune into your body and drop out of your mind—which is most often the culprit in guiding you to do the things you think you have to do as opposed to doing the things you truly desire doing—the more natural the flow you'll experience.

THE GIFT OF RECEIVING

As empaths we are naturally conditioned to give to others most often before we learn to give to ourselves. Hence empaths usually need to reverse engineer all they've learned when it comes to receiving and cultivating an equal, reciprocal flow of exchange in all relationships.

So, what does it mean to receive, exactly? Well, what first comes to mind when you hear the term? What associations do you have with the concept of receiving? Herein lies some beautiful insight to support your journey in which you, again, are you own best guide with all the perfect answers you're seeking within you.

Whatever we are waiting for—peace of mind, contentment, grace, the inner awareness of Simple Abundance—it will surely come to us, but only when we are ready to receive it with an open and grateful heart.
—Sarah Ban Breathnach, *Simple Abundance: A Daybook of Comfort*

Another de-conditioning that may be required upon starting to strengthen your receiving muscles is to let go of the transactional nature of giving and receiving that you have likely been operating under for far too long. In the society I grew up in, we are all taught from such a young age to view so many things in our lives as transactions—tit for a tat, eye for an eye, if you give me something, then I automatically owe you something. For empaths, this can manifest in many ways, but most notably as resentment at others for not giving back to you in the ways you've given freely to them. Have you been keeping score or keeping a tally of all you've given and to whom? Have you been keeping tabs on who's returned your favors and who hasn't? How's that working for you?

Time to flip the script and take back your power in yet another beautiful, liberating way, which simply starts with committing to receiving. Forget your tendency to want to give and give so much of yourself that you end up exhausted; those days are over. You have permission right this moment to drop into a new paradigm in which your primary objective is to receive all the love and support and guidance that's available to you in every moment. It's time to become a radically powerful cocreator with the infinite universe.

WHAT DO YOU WANT TO RECEIVE?

To live as a truly empowered empath, you'll soon understand that truly taking care of yourself in all the ways you deserve inherently requires you to be adept at receiving. If receiving feels challenging for you perhaps because you're so accustomed to giving to everyone else first, a beautiful place to start is by giving yourself what you truly desire first and foremost.

I am responsible for what happens to me. I receive what I have asked for.
—*A Course in Miracles*

Start making a conscious effort to spend time with yourself to get to know yourself more deeply. What do you truly enjoy about your life? What lights you up? Have you ever had a loving conversation with yourself to learn more about what feels good for you? Try practicing by asking yourself the following questions throughout your day (you can even set a timer on your phone to pop up with reminders—every thirty minutes to start is great—if that's helpful):

- What feels good for me to give myself in this moment?
- What would I most enjoy experiencing right now?
- How can I honor myself and support my highest good right now?

When was the last time you took yourself on a solo date adventure? Have you ever done such a thing? It used to be impossible for me to want to spend time alone with myself; I was so dependent on other people being around me to feel safe and distracted from my own overwhelming emotional, energetic experience. Being alone was too intense and my mind felt too loud. I didn't want to sit still long enough for it to go on overdrive, so I felt better off constantly moving and distracting myself with activities and busyness as much as possible.

As I consciously learned to love spending time with me, as I truly understood that I am the most important person in my life (and who better to spend time with than me!), my ability to receive love and support from others without any expectations became incredibly strong. As my own self-worth increased through a relentless integration of the practices mentioned throughout this book, my channels for receiving expanded beyond anything I could have possibly imagined.

Receiving is your natural state of being, even if it doesn't feel like it at this point. You are wired to operate within a divinely guided flow in which you are completely open to receiving the infinite guidance and intuitive hints you're meant to manifest. As your receiving muscles are strengthened, your self-worth and self-esteem will be intrinsically healed, further empowering your ability to trust your all-powerful intuition and take aligned action in service to your highest good. This is how you live in a continuous state of win-win. Your embodiment of your highest good supports the highest good of the collective, contributing to harmony and balance on a mass level. You—your happiness, fulfillment, and alignment—are so important to the whole.

EXERCISE: STRETCH YOUR RECEIVING MUSCLES

What's it like to feel as good as you can possibly feel? More supported than ever before? More tuned into your desires than you've ever known possible? Get ready to indulge. Today your assignment is to receive, and then receive some more. Create (identify, find, allow, notice, etc.) at least three opportunities throughout your day today in which you can receive support, help, something you want, one of your desires, someone taking something off your plate, or—even better—someone deliberately helping you with something.

Here are a few examples of what this could look like (and I strongly encourage you to stretch yourself beyond your comfort zone as much as possible):

- Ask a stranger to buy you a coffee or a drink at the store, just because. See what happens.
- Ask someone at work to do something for you that you normally do yourself. It doesn't matter how big or small it is.
- Ask someone to take a task or obligation off your plate for the day just because you want to create free time to luxuriate on your own—again, just because.
- Ask for a day off this week to relax. Or better yet, declare you are taking a day off this week and then ask for help in clearing your schedule, whatever that may entail.
- Ask someone for fare on public transportation (even if you have your own).
- Ask the restaurant where you are ordering something to make something off the menu just for you, in a specific way you like it. *Notice if you experience the inclination to not want to inconvenience anyone.*

- Where else do you go throughout your day where you can ask for something specifically the way you want it, even if it doesn't exist as an option? Where can you create a new option for you that best aligns to your needs?
- Cancel something that you don't want to do or that doesn't align with your deepest desires.
- Ask someone on the bus or train if you can have his seat just to experience what it's like to be given to in this regard. Receive it without any guilt.
- Ask someone to clean something up for you just because you want it to be cleaned. Then enjoy the experience of having this done for you.

How did that feel for you? Was setting yourself up with opportunities to receive more challenging or easy? Were you willing to stretch yourself beyond your comfort zone? Most importantly, are you willing to continue showing up for this practice? Start from where you are, and always remember to check in with yourself to re-engage your commitment.

Why does the art of receiving matter? It matters because when you are open to receiving, you are more receptive to allowing the magical flow of life to guide you as you listen to your powerful intuition.

THE GIFT OF CREATING HEALTHY BOUNDARIES WITH YOUR ENERGY

You can probably easily remember times in which you entered into a social situation and felt incredibly drained afterward. How about feeling sad, distraught, worried, fearful, or some other kind of emotion whose source within yourself you can't quite place?

Have you ever noticed your tendency to attract relationships wherein people are suffering and come to you for refuge and support? Sometimes it can feel like just by simply being in your presence the sufferer experiences relief. But are you exhausted after these kinds of interactions? If so, chances are you just encountered an energy vampire who was likely unconsciously preying on your storehouse of positive, loving energy in order to fill his or her own lacking source within.

BOUNDARIES STOP ENERGY VAMPIRES

Of course, not everyone is conscious of their roles in these kinds of interactions. I know I wasn't for most of my life. But I attracted codependent relationships, one after the other, including a recurring pattern of intimate partnerships in which I always wanted to save or fix my significant others because I saw their true potential and deeply desired helping them reach it. Herein lies another gift of highly empathic people: we have the ability to see the best in everyone, which underpins our deep love for the world and all living things. We can see what others are really capable of, and we can't help but constantly entertain what it would be like if only they could see it in themselves. Subconsciously, it can be common to take on the responsibility of trying to bring out the best in as many people as possible, particularly in intimate partners. Without any energetic boundaries established or any understanding of energetic sovereignty being key to true intimacy, our relationships can be immensely challenging to navigate.

My relationships for much of my early experiences mirrored a recurring pattern in which I would find partners and truly fall in love with their full brilliant potential that I saw so clearly, instead of with whom they were in the present moment. Then I would take it upon myself to help them see themselves and really rise to their full potential, often times losing myself in the process. I'd fall into the familiar pattern of letting the other person become the focal point of my entire life, the central motivator of my purpose and all my energy. As long as I felt needed and loved, I felt fulfilled. But there was always a draining sensation underlying these relationships that would continue until I learned how energetic boundaries are crucial to allowing the kinds of connections I deeply desire and deserve to take shape.

What are boundaries and why else, in addition to what's already been mentioned, are they important to living a thriving, empowered life? As Cyndi Dale writes in *Energetic Boundaries*, "Just as our physical body is protected by our skin, our psyche and spirit have 'energetic boundaries' that keep out harmful influences. These boundaries, invisible to the naked eye, are more than just defenses; these 'spiritual borders' are our soul's way of communicating to the universe what we do and don't want to experience in life." Boundaries are essential to ensuring our individual well-being on multiple levels. With clear boundaries we can discern with ease and focused consciousness all the good things we desire inviting into our lives while simultaneously shielding ourselves from attracting anything or anyone that doesn't serve us.

In fact, the entire notion of shielding or protection actually becomes a moot point once you establish clear boundaries because you naturally fall out of resonance with all people, places, opportunities, and the like that don't align with your optimal well-being. When you are consciously choosing to allow into your energy field the elements of life that empower you fully to be the loving being that you are, all else that isn't in support of that natural flow simply falls away. Such is the natural law of the universal flow of energy.

One of the most powerful practices for well-being you can integrate—and the more often the better, especially at first—is to strategically sharpen your awareness around how you are showing up energetically in all areas of your life. In the following exercise you'll learn a powerful practice for creating strong boundaries that will instantly empower you to become more familiar with what being in your own energy feels like and how to cultivate even stronger discernment of foreign influences or obstructions.

YOUR ENERGETIC BOUNDARIES EMPOWER OTHERS

Imagine if we all learned how to protect our energy from day one, or if there was a class in elementary school dedicated to supporting us in creating clear energetic boundaries! I love envisioning a future in which our collective education includes precisely these kinds of tools and methodologies for helping us embody our optimal states of well-being.

In the meantime you can rest easy knowing that as you practice your own cultivation of clear, healthy energetic boundaries, you empower others to act more responsibly with their own energy too. We really are such powerful mirrors for one another. Imagine if just by being in your presence, witnessing your strength, firm grounding, and independence, you inspire others to investigate how they themselves can incorporate a deepened commitment to self-care, awareness, and consciousness into their daily life.

THE GIFT OF TRUSTING YOUR INTUITION

We have all heard the term *intuition*, as it's been used colloquially in so many forms, but have you ever stopped to really consider what it actually means? The two most frequently referenced definitions are:

- The ability to understand something immediately, without thinking about it.
- The power to know something without obviously learning it beforehand.

EXERCISE: CREATING STRONG ENERGETIC BOUNDARIES

Let's practice clearing your energy field using an aura-shielding protection visualization (see Chapter 4 for more). You'll also learn how to do this clearing practice anytime you feel like your boundaries have been crossed. Take some deep breaths, get centered, and allow your intuition to guide you as you journal on the following reflections:

- Can you clearly sense what it feels like to be within your own energy field?
- Have you ever felt other people crossing into your energy or overstepping energetic boundaries with you before?
- How did you know this was happening? How did that feel?

Throughout your day, maintain awareness of your energy field (set an alert on your phone to remind yourself to check in if it helps), especially as you come into contact with others. You can do this by simply asking yourself: *how is my energy feeling? Have I absorbed anything from my environment or interactions? Am I carrying anything that is not mine?*

If you feel like you've absorbed anything that doesn't belong to you, do the aura-shielding exercise in Chapter 4. In your physical interactions with others in particular, ask yourself: am I holding myself powerfully? Standing up tall? Heart open? Shoulders back? The more powerfully and confidently you carry yourself, the less likely it is for others to penetrate your space. Do the shield-clearing exercise at the end of each day. Use the guidance provided thus far, or try creating your own visualization or meditation to help you feel cleansed and clear.

Be a conscious observer throughout this practice and take note of any insights, learnings, challenges, and surprises that would be wise to share or receive support around. Most of all, have fun and celebrate feeling your authentic energetic presence.

You might think that's two ways of saying essentially the same thing, but you catch the ultimate drift: intuition is your inherent power to simply know what is right (and wrong). It's the internal guidance system that's always directing you toward your highest alignment, your highest excitement, and a pleasure-filled life rooted in love and service.

I've personally always been vaguely aware of intuition as a concept but didn't become clear on how it related to me and my life until consciously starting to take care of myself and awakening to my true gifts and purpose here on the planet. Prior to then I was living rather unconsciously, blotting out what I perceived to be an overwhelming emotional experience with anything outside of myself that could serve as a distraction: substances, relationships, prestige, material possessions, achievements, and the like.

What I didn't know during this time was that I was actually experiencing my incredibly activated intuition guiding me away from so many of the things I was involved in that really weren't serving me—*that* was what was so overwhelming in my head; it was too much. I experienced this overwhelm as a result of living in a way that was largely guided by following my logical mind and what I understood to be practical, as opposed to living from my heart and soul's true desires.

Only in hindsight am I able to understand this dynamic. At the time I didn't know any better, as following my mind's practicality seemed to be a smart way of taking care of myself. But through that outlook I was allowing all the lifetimes and years of conditioning and imposed social order to impact (and in most cases directly influence) my decisions and actions. You can imagine how painful that must have been. I felt trapped in my mind but paradoxically didn't know that I had any other alternative available to me to feel free—I didn't know that I had another way to live, a way that could be guided by my heart and soul. I didn't trust myself enough to listen that deeply, and frankly I was scared that if I did listen, perhaps I wouldn't like what I heard. Or even worse, what I heard would be so powerful and ring so true in my heart that I would have no choice

EXERCISE: USE YOUR SENSES TO ACTIVATE YOUR INTUITION

Your intuition operates through your beautiful body's wisdom and is expressed more clearly as you tune into deeper levels of feeling. You can do this through strengthening your various sensory instruments. A powerful way to accelerate your intuitive awareness is to commit to experiencing more expansive expressions of pleasure. So get ready to invite more illustrious pleasure into your life, starting with a superpowered intention of cultivating deep joy and multisensory experiences of whatever nourishes you the most.

Take a moment to reflect on the following questions (even better if you write your responses in your journal):

- What is your favorite way to delight in your senses?
- Which sense of yours do you feel is the most developed: sight, touch, hearing, smell, taste, or intuition?
- Which senses would you like to allow more space to expand and refine?
- Which senses give you the most pleasure when you experience them deeply?

Here is your exercise:

1. Do at least one thing today that is solely for the purpose of allowing yourself to be completely immersed in pleasure.
2. Do the thing you've been meaning to do, but haven't gotten around to—a massage, a sumptuous snack, a beautiful pedicure, a beauty treatment, an energy healing. Something just for you that allows you the time and space to luxuriate in your beautiful body and senses.

3. As you're enjoying this gift you've given yourself, tune into your senses along the way.
4. Consciously reflect: What are you seeing, hearing, tasting, feeling, intuiting, smelling? Tune in and really focus on your senses. What feels good? What feels great? What do you want more of?
5. Listen to all your beautiful intuitive insights that come as soon as you allow yourself space to relax and rejuvenate.

After your experience, you likely have new information to support your continued intuitive empowerment. Recall what feels the best and consider how you can integrate more of that experience into your everyday life going forward.

Give yourself permission to luxuriate and fall deeply in love with the full spectrum of sensory experiences you've been gifted with in your beautiful, one-of-a-kind human body, a vehicle of pure divine expression.

but to listen and actually take the action I was being guided to take, even if it was directly opposed to what my mind would have me do instead.

My entire journey with trusting my intuition has been one of dropping out of my mind and into my heart, body, and soul. I learned from such a young age to listen to my mind over all else. It wasn't my fault, of course; as an ultrasensitive empath I was absorbing so much of this mind-centered way of being from the collective consciousness and cultural conditioning, all completely rooted in logic and intellect as opposed to heart-centered feeling. I can now see how I've been set up with the absolute perfect lessons to teach me what I've come here to learn and embody to ultimately thrive and be an invitation for so many others to do the same.

TYPES OF INTUITION

Did you know that intuition operates in many different facets as far as your senses are concerned? Everyone has an intuition; that's a fact. Our bodies are designed to operate with our powerful internal guidance system leading the way; that's what we are wired for. We are like supercomputers in this way, engineered to channel infinite information and direction to support us in manifesting our deepest desires and embodying our soul missions to such expansive degrees. How exciting and high-tech! While every human comes inherently designed with the intuitive gifts and software, so-to-speak, to utilize it, your gifts may manifest in one or more of the following ways with particularly strong potency:

- CLAIREMPATHY (CLEAR EMOTION): This is actually another way of describing the empath experience, particularly denoting how empaths are able to tune into the energy and emotions of other living beings, the collective consciousness, and other vibrational content.
- CLAIRSENTIENCE (CLEAR SENSATION OR FEELING): Many empaths identify with being clairsentient as well, which indicates an ability to receive intuitive, psychic insight through feeling and

sensation communicated by the entire body. If you can feel what someone else is feeling and simply know the reason why or understand it, you are utilizing clairsentience.

- CLAIRCOGNIZANCE (CLEAR KNOWING): If you've ever had a gut feeling or simply known about something that was going to happen without any evidence, you're tuning into claircognizance. You may receive simple insights about people and situations occasionally, or you may receive downloaded ideas.

- CLAIRTANGENCY (CLEAR TOUCHING): This expression is also commonly referred to as psychometry. If you've ever held an object or touched an area with your palms and received information about the owner of the object or its history that was previously unknown, you're tuning into clairtangency.

- CLAIRGUSTANCE (CLEAR TASTING): If you've ever been able to taste something without actually having it in your mouth to literally taste, you are accessing your clairgustance abilities. According to QuantumPossibilities.biz, "those who possess this ability are able to perceive the essence of a substance from the spiritual or ethereal realms through taste."

- CLAIRAUDIENCE (CLEAR HEARING): According to PsychicLibrary .com, "Clairaudience, which means clear hearing, is the ability to perceive sounds or words from outside sources in the spirit world. Psychics who are clairaudient hear voices, sounds or music that are not audible to the normal ear. They receive these messages mentally or within their ears."

- CLAIRVOYANT (CLEAR VISION): If you've ever had a vision of a past, present, or future occurrence or received information internally as through viewing a picture or movie within your consciousness, you are tuning into clairvoyance. When you hear about your third eye being open to receive visions, this is another reference to clairvoyance. QuantumPossibilities.biz explains that "a clairvoyant is one who

The Empath Experience

receives extrasensory impressions, and symbols in the form of 'inner sight' or mental images which are perceived without the aid of the physical eyes and beyond the limitations of ordinary time and space."

- CHANNELING: According to QuantumPossibilities.biz, channeling happens when someone "allows his/her body and mind to be used as a mechanism for etheric world intelligence to bring psychic information or healing energy to others." It occurs when a channel allows "an etheric world intelligence to enter one's mind and impress thoughts upon the consciousness to be spoken aloud, using one's voice or body to deliver the information or healing energy."

I actually believe we are all channels. Regardless of where you believe you fall on the intuitive scale and regardless of where you may be on your awakening path, in my experience we are all wired to be channels of the divine intuition we've been gifted. When you're operating as a channel of higher guidance and wisdom to come through you, you transcend time and space (which only exist in logical, linear understanding) and feel what it is like to be fully utilized in the fullest expression of your unique soul gifts.

Now that you know about the different ways your intuition can be experienced—and these are just a few of our known expressions, as there are infinite ways your intuition communicates—which ones do you relate to if any? Are there particular areas of your intuitive expression that you'd like to develop further? Listen to your internal guidance and tune into how you can best support yourself in sharpening your skills in a way that feels good for you. Which expression feels fun and exciting?

Trust that any and all of these expressions are available to all human beings and can be learned with practice along with a commitment to self-care, nourishment, and living life in alignment with your highest good in all possible ways. How beautiful to imagine the infinite expressions of our intuitive selves. There are as many expressions as there are human beings on the planet!

JOE'S EMPATH EXPERIENCE

I've always been aware of my intuition at least as a concept, but it became strikingly apparent that I would do well to really heed its guidance when I had a brutal concussion in 2013. My accident prompted me to learn how to slow down—which is something I realized I had never really learned how to do. For example, the day after my accident I thought it would be safe to go DJ for a night. It took my doctor telling me straightforwardly to do absolutely nothing and rest—as in, black out my lights, lie in bed, and sleep for a few days—to finally slow down. After this rest period I was feeling well enough to return to a semblance of a normal life.

Later on I was on the train going to work and found myself amidst the morning rush of everyone speeding on their way to get to wherever they needed to go and I instantaneously took that energy on and followed suit, starting my own rush into the office. Shortly thereafter I realized how rushing brought back my concussion symptoms with a vengeance. I learned from this experience that rushing and moving too fast was having a negative effect on my body while altogether disconnecting me from my intuition, which was operating through my body's clear ability to communicate.

After this experience I became much more conscious of my body's rhythms, which subsequently lead me to strengthen my connection to my own intuition and now informs the way I live my life. I listen to my body and let my intuition speak to me through my body's inherent wisdom. I don't get concussion headaches when I rush these days, but I am grateful to know that my optimal state of being is cultivated when I take time to slow down, listen to how I am feeling, and honor my natural rhythm.

THE GIFT OF TRUSTING YOUR BODY

If you've had a hard time being in your body until now, are you willing to cultivate a new experience? Let's dive in together. For empaths it may be challenging to feel safe being in your body, especially if you've learned early on to be out of your body to avoid feeling the full spectrum of your sensory experience that's thus far been too overwhelming. But becoming completely empowered in your empathic gifts not only requires being in your body, but also enjoying your bodily sensory experience as much as possible.

THE PAIN OF DISCONNECTION FROM YOUR BODY

You might experience intense challenges when it comes to trusting your body, wanting to be in your body at all, and connecting intimately in sexual situations that require genuine, authentic presence and honest communication. Here are some other instances that might resonate when it comes to empaths and sexuality:

- Especially when it comes to sex, you may have had a particularly traumatic experience in sexual encounters or with understanding how your own sexuality is expressed; you may feel really disconnected from your own body and the ability to truly intimately connect with another person on this level.
- You might have experienced sex as completely living through the other person's body/feelings instead of in your own. Because you're disconnected from your own experience and body altogether, you don't allow yourself to feel pleasure in the ways you actually desire.
- This suppression of your own pleasure experience can result in energetic blocks in other areas of your life, including creativity, living in your purpose, and cultivating abundance.

For much of my life I didn't want to be in my body. I didn't know it at the time, of course. I wasn't consciously deciding to be out of my body—I was just drawn to activities and escapisms that would take me out of myself so I could mute my intense senses that were manifesting as a very heavy weight to carry on my shoulders. But I remember when I was a younger child truly delighting in my senses. I loved moving and feeling my body, smelling flowers, tasting delicious food, and most of all, being affectionate with people I loved.

Something switched notably around adolescence when my developmental hormones started kicking in and my self-consciousness turned all the way up. It was around the time that I was entering middle school that my empathic sensitivity was extremely heightened and activated to a new degree, more intensely than ever before. I suddenly became extremely uncomfortable in my body, a challenge that manifested in a multitude of burdens I would go on to carry for the next decade.

I believe I had a heightened sense of body dysmorphia, which means I saw things on my body, such as stretch marks and imperfections in the overall shape of my body and face, that weren't actually indicative of how I appeared in reality. My perspective of how I saw myself in the mirror was incredibly tainted by the deeply rooted ideas I had about what was wrong with me based on what I saw in advertising and airbrushed photos of models with perfect skin, perfect teeth, and absolutely not a single thing out of place. I remember spending hours in the mirror wondering how I would ever get rid of the stretch marks that kept appearing as I continued to go through a seemingly never-ending growth spurt. I was always the tallest girl in class up until almost eighth grade, and to make matters worse I had stretch marks on the insides of my knees to prove it.

At the time I was also likely absorbing everyone else's adolescent insecurities on high alert around me, further amplifying my own sensitivity and self-criticism. My feeling of not being enough was incredibly amplified, and I was obsessed about my appearance, particularly what kind of clothes I should wear in order to feel like I fit in at school. I also got really addicted to the Internet, instant messaging, and creating websites so I could zone out completely instead of picking myself apart in the mirror, dissecting all my imperfections—as though by doing so I could magically fix everything that I felt was wrong.

Everything changed when I first got drunk, and by no coincidence whatsoever, on the same night I also had my first intense make-out session with not one, but two guys at a house party. From then on alcohol in particular became an important part of my life as far as intimate relationships and feeling safe to be in my body were concerned. As long as I was buzzed or drunk I wasn't so overwhelmed by what everyone was feeling or thinking about me, so I genuinely felt like I could enjoy myself and connect with people I was attracted to, be adventurous, and tune into my sensual side that was dying to be expressed.

A key paradox of my journey this far, which is perhaps applicable to your journey as well, is that while all I truly want in life is deep, genuine connection and a feeling of being truly seen for who I am, I am the only thing in my way of receiving that because of my equally powerful fear of rejection if I am in fact truly seen. Never has this paradox become more evident as in my sexual experiences. Sex for empaths can come with an array of challenges, some of which may feel painful to even illuminate if you've been hiding out for years, like I did in relationship after relationship.

I didn't lose my virginity until I was eighteen, which at the time I felt was really late in the game compared to everyone else I knew. But the fact is, I didn't know myself at all and was so programmed to live through the eyes of others—disconnected from my body, from my intuition, and most of all, from my true desires—that I couldn't express what I wanted and I was conditioned to perform like I was acting in a show simply for someone else's viewing pleasure. And of course, how you show up for sex is how you show up for the rest of your life—which was precisely the case for me over the following decade after first losing my virginity.

Quite honestly, I felt for years that something was wrong with me because my body didn't seem to work the same as how I saw women in porn or in popular culture acting. I wasn't having orgasms on demand within minutes or having ecstatic experiences of release and pleasure with little preparation—no, my experience couldn't be further from that scene actually.

On the contrary, I learned to fake orgasms for years and years, in very serious relationships even, because I learned to perform for my partner. I could feel that they were attached to pleasuring me, not because they cared about me, but to validate their own accomplishment in doing so—and I had to give them what they wanted. I had to perform and give them what I knew they were expecting; otherwise they might feel bad when they discovered that they couldn't please me or even know how to please me (which was further complicated by the fact that I didn't really know what was pleasurable to my body anyway because I was so disconnected).

Of course, it makes perfect sense in hindsight that I was experiencing blocks to intimacy because I actually didn't trust myself first and foremost, and subsequently I didn't truly trust many of my early partners. Real intimacy requires deep trust in yourself and your partner and the willingness to face the shadows and blocks within each of you. Such is the nature of a true sacred partnership (which, by the way, we are all designed to experience).

For the purposes of empath empowerment through trusting your body, it's absolutely crucial to get honest with yourself about how open you are to intimacy and being seen, especially in sexual situations. I only relatively recently became conscious of how my empathic nature, my intuition, and really my soul at the deepest level are so connected to my experience in intimacy, sexuality, and ultimately all areas of my life. I didn't have a real orgasm with another person as my witness in an intimate exchange until I was twenty-eight, and even after that experience I was ashamed to speak about it because I was still carrying the weight of societal expectations and wearing a mask based on what I thought other people wanted to see.

Low self-worth was another underlying factor of this perpetuated cycle—even though it was subtly operating at a low level, it was still draining me enormously and preventing me from fully showing up in the powerful essence I am truly here to embody. I didn't believe I deserved to experience pleasure to the full extent that my body was capable of receiving. I was also afraid of being seen in my most authentic expression of power—which, if you think about it, is conveyed through the body's ability to communicate its life force essence through orgasm. I was terrified of my own power, so much so that I felt like if I actually unleashed the floodgates of the energy and emotion I sensed was underlying the years and years of repression I would surely implode as well as scare away whomever I was choosing to let in on the experience.

HOW TO LOVE AND TRUST YOUR BODY

As empaths in particular, we have access to such a profoundly broad spectrum of sensation ripe with inherent intuitive wisdom. Our invitation is to fully rise into our highest embodiment of pleasure, bliss, and joy so we can be the clear channels that we are designed to be for sharing our completely unique gifts with the world. Essentially, our job is joy. As long as you follow that principle above all else, you are taken care of in every way imaginable—including loving and trusting your body. It really is that simple.

So how can you become fully empowered in your sexuality and pleasure embodiment? As I've mentioned elsewhere, you start by asking for what *you* truly want. Here are some other suggestions:

- Spend time taking care of yourself sensually, getting to know your body and what feels good. This is one of the most healing things you can do for yourself—nurturing yourself by treating yourself like someone you deeply love and care for.

- Initiate a practice of self-massage with aromatherapy and essential oils. Sending energy healing to parts of you that feel neglected or desire touch is a beautiful way to start.
- In intimate relationships, practice using truthful, authentic communication in every possible opportunity that arises. Can you communicate with precision what you are feeling and experiencing in every moment, especially during sexual encounters? You may need to push past any fear of being seen in this level of transparency to do so.

So much freedom awaits you on the other side of taking the leap. Start from where you are and ask for help if you need it. Remember, you don't ever have to hide and you never have to do anything alone. You have a community of empaths to support you!

JEAN'S EMPATH EXPERIENCE

I faked orgasms for years, even in serious relationships, and my partners never knew that I was faking it. I know now that all along I was hurting myself deeply. I didn't trust my body whatsoever. I was living for other people completely. Ultimately I caused myself so much physical, emotional, and spiritual pain as a result of not expressing myself and not feeling safe to release the energy within me that wanted so badly to be released.

I actually experienced the physical ramifications of this painful cycle, which manifested as a recurring inflammatory response rendered in my Bartholin's glands, which are lymph nodes on either side of the vagina. I used to be so ashamed of speaking about this, carrying so much shame in secret about what I thought to be true about myself: there's something really wrong with my body and it simply doesn't work right.

Yet I knew at a deeper level the injury I was experiencing was just a physical manifestation of the energy I was blocking from being released from within my system. The blocked energy materialized as these literally blocked glands that became inflamed and incredibly painful to the point where I would go to urgent care and see doctors in secret, so terribly embarrassed that this was my reality—and I'd never tell my partners what was going on. Talk about suffering in silence. To make matters worse, some doctors I worked with over the years didn't even know what my condition was or how to treat it. I sensed at a deeper level it was my fault and that the injury was due to my own inability to express myself in my truth. As long as I was unwilling to be seen for who I really am, in my fullest expression of power, I continued to experience this recurring blockage.

I finally came to terms with my truth, which is that I must put myself first no matter what, above all else, in order to live a truly empowered, happy life. I'm so grateful for my experiences because now I have such a deep appreciation and respect for intimacy and what it really requires.

DISCOMFORT ALWAYS LEADS TO GROWTH

How have I become truly empowered to trust and love my body and all its power? Well, as with most lessons in my life, after experiencing so much pain and repression—pain is certainly a touchstone of spiritual growth in my case—I surrendered and asked for help. I was over the self-perpetuated suffering I had been creating. With the help of a mentor I hired to support me across business, spirituality, and energetic mastery, I was guided to stand in radical truth and communicate publicly about the things I was most ashamed of people knowing about me. I shared in a *Facebook Live* stream—that was viewed by almost two thousand people—the entire story of my repressed sexual expression and how years of hiding my truth in intimate situations manifested as huge blocks to my creative expression in other areas of my life.

I then became willing to release the charge I had still within me around any shame or guilt—both of which are the most toxic energies we can possibly ever carry in our beings (and which I also believe to be the source of many physical manifestations of illnesses). I became willing to go to any lengths to be truly seen. I wanted to occupy a space of radical truth no matter what, at any expense, especially at the expense of appearing to look like a fool—my biggest fear.

As I continued to push through my fears and share my radically authentic, sometimes shocking truth, I experienced the biggest growth in my business I could ever have imagined possible. My expression was so magnetic that I instantly attracted more clients who wanted to work with me as well as more opportunities that brought with them incredible abundance. It was then that I truly began to experience the power of tuning into my body's truth no matter what—trusting that my body absolutely holds the answers to everything I could ever dream of wanting or experiencing. I was finally listening.

I am continuing to unravel more and more around this specific relationship between my body's wisdom and intuitive knowledge, intimacy, pleasure, power, and authentic expression (and how all of these concepts are immensely connected to all levels of abundance in the material plane), but I am so proud of how far I have come.

THE GIFT OF MANIFESTING YOUR DESIRES

Empaths are skilled at manifesting (the art of speaking and feeling your desires into being) because the central component to manifesting successfully is feeling. When you are attuned to feeling the emotional experience of any situation you could possibly imagine, you have a potent recipe for manifesting your wildest dreams. However, if you've been manifesting less than ideal situations thus far, and you feel as though life perhaps isn't flowing your way, it's time to take your power back yet again and get back in the driver's seat.

EXERCISE: ACTIVATE YOUR PLEASURE SENSE

What comes to mind when you hear the word *pleasure*? Take a moment to reflect on what comes up for you. Do you affiliate that word with a particular kind of experience, circumstance, person, place, or thing? Pleasure is actually your divine empathic superpower. It's your key to tuning into what is fully in resonance with your soul's deepest desires, and with what your intuition is guiding you to experience and cultivate.

Your assignment is to regularly tune into your sensory experience and consciously allow yourself to receive more pleasure (and practice giving it to yourself). Here's your exercise:

1. Set an alarm on your phone to go off each hour to remind you to tune in. Starting now. Alternatively, remind yourself to check in every hour for at least three minutes to do the following body scan and pleasure attunement practice.

2. During your check-in time, close your eyes, breathe deeply, and consciously tune into your body sensations. Ask yourself: how do I feel in this moment? How is my energy feeling? What do I deeply desire? What would feel most pleasurable right now?

3. Listen to whatever intuitive insights you receive. If you feel that you need something to support you, can you give yourself whatever that may be? If you deeply desire something in this moment, how can you provide this for yourself?

4. Use your imagination and allow yourself to be creative with how you give yourself what you need. What would be a stretch? Can you honor your deepest desires to feel pleasure, love, and support in this moment? How far are you willing to go to allow yourself to feel as amazing as possible?

5. Journal what's come up for you today during this practice. How did you give yourself what you need? What was fun? What was challenging? What have you learned?
6. Notice any resistance that comes up along the way. Taking note of the beliefs, thoughts, fears, and blocks in your journal. Are there any specific beliefs that arise? What are they? What feelings emerge when you tune in to allow yourself to receive what you truly desire?

True intimacy and pleasure are amplified when you are able to cultivate those things within yourself first and foremost. As with everything else you've learned thus far, your most incredible empowered state imaginable is always an "inside job." Start from within and quickly thereafter watch your external world align more perfectly than ever to support you in precisely the ways you desire most.

UNDERSTANDING MANIFESTATION

You may hear *manifestation* referred to in magazine and web articles—it is a major buzzword, particularly in spiritual communities and within the new age circuit. Perhaps you've heard of Abraham–Hicks Law of Attraction or watched the film *The Secret*, which is credited with bringing the magic of manifestation to the masses through a more scientific, practical lens. Regardless of your familiarity or even belief in the concept of manifestation, above all else the fact is that as energetic beings, we as humans are constantly speaking, feeling, and thinking our realities into being.

What an empowered stance to take! You are radically responsible for your experience in every way—you are, in fact, creating it. How beautiful does it feel to know that you have the power to change your circumstances? Isn't it empowering to know that life is actually happening *for* you, out of your own creation as opposed to the alternative (that life is happening to you and you have no influence over your experiences)?

Empaths take manifestation to another, much more heightened level with the potential for a nearly instantaneous impact through their unique ability to embody such potent emotions, more so than a person who is less energetically sensitive. If you're an empath and you've been experiencing less than ideal manifestations in your life, it's quite possible that you're creating your reality with far too much influence from what other people around you are feeling, saying, and thinking.

Have you ever felt like you're experiencing life as though it's not actually your life? Similar to whether you've ever felt like you've experienced other people's emotions instead of your own, your subsequently materializing life events can feel just the same if you're holding other people's realities instead of your own.

RECLAIMING YOUR POWER

Much like we've already discussed throughout our journey together thus far, you have an opportunity right now to take back your power and claim the reality that you most desire. You deserve it. And as an empath, you are uniquely gifted with the ability to harness your gifts to create powerful, instantaneous manifestations reflecting your optimal alignment. You are so supported in bringing precisely what you desire into being. The more you create in alignment with your soul's purpose, the more you contribute to the entire collective's harmonious coexistence and natural balance.

Your desires are your keys to life. Your passion and whatever it is that brings you the most joy above everything else is certainly not random—it's your golden key to unlocking your soul's map of purpose and power in your life. Once you can fully own your desires and clearly claim them as your divine right to receive, you will easily receive the intuitive guidance on what actions you can take in life that will support you in embodying your ideal alignment. By now you know that tuning into your desires starts with taking care of yourself no matter what. That's why establishing self-love, trust, and worthiness empowers you to be able to listen to the intuitive insight you receive through your body's wisdom. Once you are more adept at listening, then the fun starts—you get to take big, expansive action in your life that aligns to your desires, unlocking a beautiful potent flow of divine synchronicity that I can't wait for you to experience.

Manifestation is rather simple when you are clearly listening and acting accordingly. That's what alignment ultimately implies—it's another way to understand integrity, which presupposes that your actions, beliefs, and feelings are completely integrated to the highest possible degree. The greater your integrity, the greater alignment you will experience in your life. In this arena you will understand what the concept of "quantum leaping" really means, as you come to embody it more fully in infinite ways—collapsing results that used to take you a year or more to manifest into a matter of days, weeks, or even hours.

When you strike your ideal alignment and live in optimal integrity, completely fueled by your razor-sharp, passion-filled vision, you will see firsthand how supported you are by the entire universe in living the life you've always dreamed of for yourself. It all starts with knowing you deserve it and then, as we've discussed, continuing your conditioning work to make sure you are open to receiving all the gifts that will surely be sent your way to enjoy. You are so powerful. Your emotions are creating your reality in this moment. What are you allowing to be expressed? The more conscious you can be of what you're infusing into your reality via your thoughts and feelings, the more you will be able to see how much immediate influence you have over your circumstances.

THE TRANSFORMATION FROM ANXIETY TO ABUNDANCE

For much of my life, when I was living unconsciously and certainly prior to identifying or owning my intuitive, empathic gifts, I was constantly experiencing chaos, fear, and a nearly continuous stream of anxiety. This was my normal state, and as I continued to allow my thoughts and feelings to live within those three emotional states, the situations and relationships I attracted were an absolute reflection of my internal uneasiness. For so long it really felt like I was caught in a downward spiral of unmanageability that would trap me in a few different behavior loops that were unpleasant...but that at the same time were comfortable in their familiarity.

Now I can see that I had become comfortable with being uncomfortable. I was comfortable with chaos, creating drama, having fires to put out, and getting into trouble in all sorts of ways—arrests, hospital visits, and accidents, to name a few. Ultimately, as a creature of habit, it was challenging for me to readjust into a more positive, healthy, integrated state of being when the time came to change because for so long I had been accustomed to low-level suffering that always required me to be on the hunt for some kind of resolution.

For a long time this was the dynamic in which I sourced my sense of purpose and fulfillment in life, but it was never actually satisfying, because I was operating in such a shallow space. I never allowed myself to access and receive the deeper truth that was dying to come through. Without a foundation of self-trust, self-worth, and self-care I wouldn't crack through the superficiality I had been so accustomed to sorting through for years on end. I have made that progress, and you can too.

I'm most excited about the power empaths have collectively to manifest a healthy, healing, happy world for all of us to enjoy and share. To dramatically raise the vibration of the entire planet and manifest ideal conditions such as world peace, environmental vibrancy, and massive abundance, Gregg Braden, author of *The Divine Matrix*, says that a relatively small percentage—close to 1 percent—of the entire global population is required to meditate, take care of themselves, and contribute positively to the collective consciousness through their positivity, spiritual practice, and healing.

With our supercharged capacity for feeling and speaking our desires into being, imagine what happens if we focus our energy on manifesting the most joyful, abundant, healthy, happy lives we can imagine! We naturally have a ripple effect on countless other beings who come into our paths and positively influence them in turn to take better care of themselves, love themselves more deeply, and, most of all, tune into what's possible for them to live life beyond their wildest dreams too.

EXERCISE: DECLARE YOUR DEEPEST DESIRES

Here's a daily practice for you to mindfully notice each choice that comes into your path throughout the day and seize all the opportunities you have to claim and manifest your deepest desires. Note how many opportunities you have to assert your preferences. Consciously reclaim your power from anything or anyone you may have been allowing to influence your truth until now. Here is your exercise:

1. Each moment that you have a preference or choice offered to you, practice checking in with yourself in that moment to ask yourself: what do I truly desire? What would serve my highest good? Which is the preference that is most nourishing for my soul?
2. Then the challenge: communicate clearly what you truly want (at work, in your relationships, in any interactions you have, literally in all possibly capacities). How powerfully can you declare your truth? How straightforwardly can you ask for what you truly desire?
3. This exercise requires you to practice with intention the art of pause. Pause, breathe, and tune in to see what you truly want, and then decide.
4. Notice any inclination you have to give your preference or choice to others or what they may need or what suits them.

Become aware of any tendency you have to tune into what another person may be feeling before checking in with how you feel first and foremost. If you notice yourself tuning into the other person's needs ahead of your own, simply bring your focus back to yourself and ask yourself what you desire in this moment.

This exercise can give you precisely what your internal guidance is leading you toward. The more consistent and intentional you are with this practice, the more easily you'll condition yourself to have a default response that always honors your needs above all else.

CHAPTER 3
Self-Care for Your Body and Mind

If you had told me that self-care would be one of the top reasons for my success in achieving everything I've ever wanted, I wouldn't have believed you. For most of my life I had always expected someone to give me an answer or guidance leading me to some solution outside of myself. I had developed an outward-facing perspective in which I learned to look to others' experience to dictate how I felt.

Before I became aware of the term *empath*, I really hadn't been taking great care of myself. Because I was born so sensitive to other's emotional states, from day one I learned some interesting survival skills in order to manage my daily experience. My survival skill lessons first started with my family. This is, after all, where we first all learn how to be in relationships. Our parents provide the template for relationships as well as the attachment strategies we will spend the rest of our lives mirroring. But of course, again, I didn't know that was the case at the time.

The first survival skill I learned as a child to mitigate the intensity of emotional information that was coming my way flowed like this:

- If other people around me are happy, then I am okay.
- If other people around me are sad, then I am not okay.
- Therefore, in order for me to be okay, other people need to be happy.
- It's up to me to make sure people are happy so I am okay.

That's how I learned to use my empathic abilities to see what other people needed to feel happy. I also subconsciously allowed myself to energetically absorb negativity, doubt, fear, worry—any of the negative emotions I sensed others would be feeling—in an attempt to help them get rid of their negative experience.

Years later, in my early twenties, when I finally learned the word *empath*, I realized I had in fact been operating like an emotional sponge. I would frequently have people tell me that I was like a dose of sunshine or that when I walked into a room or a social situation I was like an immediate vibe-raiser. I had that effect naturally, but at the time it was happening subconsciously at the expense of my own well-being because I had no idea I was operating with an underlying desire to help everyone else feel better so I could feel worthy of being happy.

YOUR JOB: SELF-CARE (A PRACTICE FOR LIFE)

Empaths are wired to be on high alert when it comes to emotional and energetic sensitivities. This intensity can come with similarly powerful weariness after a high degree of energy has been exhausted. As such, it's crucial for empaths to spend more time than the average person caring for our bodies and recentering ourselves so we can exist in our optimal state of being. You might find that you quickly become drained, exhausted, or completely paralyzed at certain points along your empath experience—particularly after giving a lot of yourself, after absorbing energy from a crowd or from an intense relationship, or from intensely feeling a painful or even ecstatic experience going on around you. Self-care is not only the answer to protecting yourself from ongoing exhaustion and feeling drained, but it's also a practice for life that will support you in feeling grounded, knowing yourself more deeply than you've ever imagined, and truly accepting and celebrating yourself as the magical being that you are.

The best things I have ever learned and practiced in my entire journey toward becoming fully empowered in my empathic abilities and gifts are all grounded in self-care, no doubt about it. Since you are the most important person in your life, it's time to start treating yourself like that. Start now. And have fun with it. Self-care is meant to be a joyful, loving experience that you can be creative with and through which you can express yourself fully. One of the most empowering things you can ever learn and strive to embody in your life is to truly be the person who can give yourself everything you've ever needed. How can you do that for yourself now?

SELF-CARE MIGHT NOT BE EASY FOR YOU AT FIRST

It isn't as easy as you might think to really commit to self-care. Though it seems like it might be fun to start taking care of yourself, there's more to it for empaths. If you've learned to live your entire life for others, to help others feel good, and to look good in order to please others, when you finally start to look inward at your own relationship with yourself, it can at first be an uncomfortable and unpleasant experience.

You might find that once you actually ascertain where you stand on the self-care front, you really have no idea where to even begin. You might also realize that you've been living as though everything has been okay all along when in fact this couldn't be further from the truth. You might see how many ways in which you've been allowing yourself to settle for less than optimal well-being in order to dim your light, play small, or fit in with whomever you find yourself surrounded by. Ask yourself this: what becomes possible for me when I finally start supporting myself in all the ways I truly desire? You might see how there is an underlying fear you've felt that if you really start taking care of yourself, you will shine at your full capacity, and then what? Will you be alone? Will people no longer understand you? Will you have to make some serious life changes?

That was the case for me. When I finally started looking inward, I didn't like what I found. It felt like I was meeting a stranger for the first time, and it wasn't a stranger I particularly wanted to spend time with. My whole life I always strove to surround myself with other people. It was around others that I felt safe. When other people were around, especially if I could take care of them and help them feel happy, I felt like I had a purpose. But once I was invited to be with myself and really take care of *me*, I realized I had no idea how to do that in peace. I didn't even know what peace felt like.

In addition, simply becoming aware of my overactive mind that was always operating on hyper-speed was incredibly scary. I had numbed that effect with alcohol for close to a decade, but now my mind was activated in full force. Getting sober from mind-altering substances showed me how intense my thought patterns were and how loud my mind was, constantly berating me for various things I wasn't doing well enough. Finally starting to listen to what was going on was overwhelming to say the least—it's no wonder I had turned to drugs and drinking to mute the noise. How was everyone else living like this? Did everyone else have this same experience as well, with their mind constantly yelling at them? I felt confused and alone.

My first iteration of self-care started with hiring a life coach, who guided me through my first Reiki sessions as well as an immensely powerful guided meditation in which I met my inner child for the first time. She helped me get on a healthy eating plan, and I even did a cleanse protocol to reset my entire body and all its inherent systems. I experienced what it felt like for the first time to wake up early with a natural internal alarm clock, and had some of the best sleep I had ever had in my life. I experienced optimal energy; I detoxified my life from unhealthy, exhausting relationships and obligations; I stopped doing everything for everyone else; and I really started intentionally cultivating a loving inner dialogue with myself. Because I fully invested in myself for the first time, I was enjoying the most incredible transformations in my life that I had ever experienced. I was awakening to my true power and purpose.

LEARN TO LOVE BEING ON YOUR OWN

Being on your own, let alone choosing to be solo, may be extraordinarily challenging for you if you're an empath that has developed the coping

EXERCISE: AMPLIFY YOUR SELF-LOVE

It's time to venture into the multiple layers in which love can manifest and be received, given, expressed, and shared. Remember, you are love. But how are you tuning into this (divine) truth moment to moment?

This is the real work.

This is presence. This is radical acceptance. This is power. When you operate from a space of love in which you simply know that you (and everyone else) is just that—love (reflecting one another, and so on)—you enter the realm of infinite possibility.

So, like everything else, it starts with you. It's an inside job. Here's your invitation to begin with a beautiful declaration of love for the most important person in your entire life: YOU. Your invitation is as follows:

1. Write a letter to yourself and celebrate how much you love yourself. Now is the time to tell yourself all the things you wish you'd heard your whole life from others. Answer the following questions and be sure to communicate to yourself in a loving, caring, celebratory tone—like you are your own loudest, proudest cheerleader:

    - What are you most proud of about yourself?
    - What are your most unique gifts, talents, and abilities?
    - What do you love about yourself (your body, your mind, your spirit, your wisdom)?
    - What are you grateful for about you and your life?
    - What else do you need to know, hear, be reassured about?

2. Once your letter is complete, what's next? You have a few choices:

    - You can hide it away and take it out sometime in the future to reread (time-capsule style).
    - You can hang it up on your wall so you spend time with it every day (maybe near a mirror).

- You can read it out loud to someone you care about so he or she can witness you in your beautiful glory.
- If you really want to stretch, ask someone you love to read the letter to you as though she is saying all the things to you...simply reading your letter aloud so you can fully receive the love.

Or...you can do all of the above! What feels best? What would be a stretch? Now's your chance to go all in. Enjoy luxuriating in your beautiful celebratory magic: you deserve it. How does it feel to receive your own medicine? Keep in mind any resistance that comes up. Your resistances and triggers are often your most profound teachers. Do you feel embarrassed at all while considering what this exercise is offering? Why might that be? Do you feel reluctant to read this out loud to someone else, to be seen? Do you feel uncomfortable allowing yourself to feel celebrated? If any of these thoughts are present for you, trust that you're absolutely right where you're supposed to be. Ask yourself where these thoughts are coming from. Are they emanating from your heart, your soul, your intuition, or from your mind? What is your actual truth? What do you actually desire experiencing deep down? How can you listen to the deeper knowing within you that wants to provide you with everything you truly want?

The more you can develop your strength and trust in yourself to witness your resistance and support yourself through receiving whatever lessons are on offer, the sooner you will start to cultivate a new relationship with fear. The more you can identify your triggers and decide to receive and integrate the divine lessons that are curated just for you, the more freedom you will experience. Ultimately as time goes you'll also become less activated by things that used to truly bother you.

Wherever you are in your process, be your own witness. Acknowledge it all, trusting it is all perfect and a sign that you're right on time. Divinely, as ever. Have fun loving YOU.

mechanism of constantly surrounding yourself with other people to distract yourself from your own emotional experience. Going solo may tune you into that loud tape set on repeat, inundating you with an intense onslaught of emotional, energetic information. You might feel overwhelmed by how loud your mind is; it might even feel scary to really listen in and discern the conversations that have been going on in the background despite your best attempts at distraction. Trust me, I've been there.

Choosing to spend more time alone is crucial for developing a stronger relationship with yourself so you can cultivate self-love, worthiness, and ultimately a clearer, more trusting understanding of your own intuition and energy. It's time to get to know yourself better than you ever imagined. Your empath superpowers are waiting to get fully activated, but doing so requires the initial foundation of learning who you are before you can really start to discern your own experience from that of anyone else's.

If the thought of starting to consciously spend time solo freaks you out, I understand. I felt the same way when I received my first assignment to try it out. But doing so ended up catalyzing the biggest growth and healing I had ever experienced. To get started, I recommend purposefully blocking out time in your schedule to see what it feels like to have unstructured free time with which you can explore your creative inspiration, take spontaneous actions in alignment with your highest excitement, or simply allow yourself to take a break and rest. Before I got comfortable with being alone I realized that I had become far too accustomed to overscheduling my life so that I barely had space to breathe. I figured that as long as I was busy I could tune out the intensity of my experiences. Overscheduling was a coping mechanism for sure.

When you start exploring what it feels like to spend time solo, you can ease into it by starting with smaller increments of time, such as an hour or two here and there, but commit to the practice at least a few days of the week—even better if you can try for longer blocks on the weekends. The more you can practice the easier it will become, until you may find one day that you deeply desire being in your own company because you are the most amazing person on the planet and there's no one you'd rather spend time with than you. Use your free open time to ask yourself what you truly need, what you desire, what you'd like to do, and then give yourself the chance to do exactly that. Challenge yourself to be present with yourself and tune into your body's cues as opposed to simply zoning out to watch TV or be on your phone. Listen to a guided meditation, go to a new fitness class, try a new healing modality, do something artistic that feeds your spirit, journal, or simply rest and relax in whatever way feels best for you. The goal is to discover what it feels like to be present with yourself, no matter how you get there.

I remember one of the early assignments from my first coach was to dedicate time on my always-filled calendar to spend time solo. I had never done anything close to that before—in fact, I had been organizing my time in complete opposition to that idea, filling my calendar weeks in advance with plans and commitments mostly involving other people. Since what felt like forever, certainly since middle school and well into my early sobriety almost fifteen years later, I had a nagging fear of being alone with myself with nothing to do. In hindsight it makes complete sense—why would I want to spend time with me if I don't actually like me? And why would I want to be alone if I was deriving my entire sense of purpose and happiness from helping others and making sure they felt taken care of? I was dependent on others to manage my own emotional experience of feeling needed, wanted, purposeful, and fulfilled. Being alone simply wasn't an option.

Starting to spend time with myself was a huge challenge. It felt like learning to walk for the first time. I have memories of spending a lot of time alone as a child. Back then I loved being with myself and playing all the games I wanted to play in the precise ways I wanted to play them. I would spend hours creating imaginary worlds and letting my dream visions take me on wild adventures in my backyard and beyond. I loved it. I can't remember what might have been going on in my mind at that time though. I certainly wasn't as worried about the state of the world or about managing the emotional experience of all the people close to me in my life.

Being alone—and enjoying it like I used to—was exactly what was required of me to step into the next phase of my life. This was my test: could I be alone with myself, and not only that, could I learn to enjoy my time while also listening to myself and truly allowing my intuition to guide me?

I didn't know at first that what I was really doing through this exercise was starting to consciously attune to my own energy and intuition, but that's precisely what was going on. In order to finally start discerning my own voice and the truth sourced from within me, I had to retreat back into my own energy, independent of any outside influences which prior to that moment had been dominating my every decision, my every thought, my every move. I was in for some real breakthroughs indeed. I was up for the task. I knew that even though this was terrifying for me to step into, it had to be done. I sensed that this wouldn't be the first or last time I would be guided to walk directly into my biggest fears with absolute courage and trust. And in fact, it was just the beginning.

Everything changed when I learned how to be okay being on my own. Trust me, it was a process, but it continues to be the most worthwhile journey I could have imagined. It's been important for me to always remember exactly that: this is a journey, and there's no destination. The point is to enjoy being right where you are. Imagine really living that. Here's your invitation.

HOW ARE YOU NOURISHING YOU?

You can't talk about being an empath without talking about how you're choosing to nourish your body. Your body is the channel through which you experience everything—and if you've been feeling other people's

EXERCISE: CREATE YOUR PERFECT SOLO SOUL-DATE

It's time to bask in your own soulful beauty in all the most magical ways. What have you always wanted to do that you've never allowed yourself to simply enjoy and go for? It is your time to go all in and have fun, just because. You deserve to have it all. So, how can you give it all to yourself, right now, no more waiting?

Celebrate you. How can you really honor all that you are in this moment and reflect on everything you've created thus far? Today is about gratitude, deep acknowledgment, and so much self-love for you, honoring your beautiful soul for being so divinely perfect in every way.

WELCOME TO THE SELF-LOVE CLUB. Today you're going on a date with the most important person in your life: YOU. Clear the calendar (if you can't do it today, then you better set a date to do this ASAP, because...why wait?). Clear as much space and time to be offline, off your phone, and away from obligations or responsibilities as possible so you can really tune into doing only what you desire for the entire day:

- Luxuriate in this wide-open possibility.
- When have you ever given yourself a whole day to simply BE?
- What would you love to do? How do you want to enjoy your time and celebrate your divine perfection? What would feel amazing to treat yourself to? Is there an adventure you've always wanted to take or something new you've always wanted to experience that you're simply waiting to press play on? Can you do it now?

Your date is all for you. You can do whatever you want. Anything goes. Try to be offline to be completely present to your needs. Really connect to your intuition to guide your decisions and actions. Play. What is it like to be completely free? Here are some options for what you can do:

- **PLAY WITH YOUR INNER CHILD.** If it's fun to imagine playing with your inner child all day—exploring outdoors, painting, molding with clay, and so on—go for it!
- **BE SPONTANEOUS.** Is it fun to *not* plan anything because your life is typically full of plans? Try going outside with no plans and simply listen to your intuition to guide your next steps—play a new game!
- **WRITE FOR HOURS.** Journal along the way and play with your intuition by asking questions and responding with stream of consciousness writing—any particular topics you'd like to explore? What happens when you create space to truly listen in and honor yourself?
- **MEDITATE.** Take some quiet time to yourself and tune into a guided meditation, or make up your own.
- **GET MOVING.** Do something active. Dance, walk, kickbox, do yoga—whatever you choose, luxuriate in the beauty of being you.
- **MAKE MANTRAS.** Create your own mantras and power statements to support you throughout your adventure. You can also use the affirmations from the Clear Your Energy and Instantly Access Inner Peace exercise in Chapter 1 throughout the day.

No matter what, have fun and follow your highest excitement. Follow whatever it is that taps you into your expansive state of joy. Receive all the gifts you've always wanted to give yourself. Celebrate yourself like you've always wanted to be celebrated. Don't wait until your birthday or another holiday to celebrate you; start showing up like you mean it—now.

And be open to it all being better than you can even imagine. Happy solo-adventuring!

energy your entire life, chances are you've experimented with turning off your feelings with food, the most readily available numbing agent we have on offer. Sugar pretends to work wonders for many of us. I've tried it all, trust me—from sugar, to alcohol, to caffeine, to processed and fried foods, and even doing an intensive cleanse regimen diet that was extremely limited but worked as a distraction from how I felt because I could instead focus my energy on controlling my every eating habit almost obsessively.

Now that you're on your way to living a truly empowered life in your empath experience, you'll likely find that how you choose to nourish yourself will automatically shift to better support you. Trust yourself to be intuitively guided to the kinds of foods and drinks that feel best for you, empower your clarity, and ignite all your desired ways of being. Experiment and investigate different protocols—and consider that you might not even need a strict regimen. Once you really cleanse your body of toxicity you'll perhaps find that you prefer to eat healthy anyway and as such, making healthy choices is actually second nature.

Over the years I've experimented with all kinds of diets and protocols usually aimed at optimizing my energy and cosmetically clearing my notoriously congested skin. Just as I am enormously sensitive to energy, my digestive system is incredibly sensitive to all toxins and stimulants, so it became clear to me that I couldn't ingest just anything without possible negative consequences. Sugar, caffeine, and processed foods have an immediately draining effect on me, whereas fresh veggies, whole grains, fresh fruit, and other healthy foods feel energizing. You'll need to figure out what works for you, and tuning into your body frequently is the best way to do that.

THE CASE FOR QUITTING ALCOHOL

If you're a sensitive empathic being, it is probably a good idea to take an honest look at your relationship to alcohol (and any other mind-altering substances, for that matter). In fact, could you consider cutting out alcohol completely? In my experience alcohol creates holes in your auric field, making you more susceptible to absorbing external energies while further weakening your ability to discern your own emotions from those of others. If you are an empath, perhaps you already have a questionable relationship with alcohol. It's also possible that you have no attachment whatsoever to alcohol, which is great if that's the case. However, it's important to consider how this substance may be affecting you negatively, even if you aren't completely aware of it.

A helpful barometer to discern whether or not alcohol has a negative effect on you is to consider if you've ever felt like the following motivations have ever incited or exacerbated your alcohol consumption:

- Have you ever started drinking because you were around people who made you feel nervous?
- Have you ever drank too much even though you consciously made a commitment to yourself earlier on that you wouldn't drink at all or that you'd limit yourself to a specific amount?
- Have you fantasized about drinking to black out so you could escape from an uncomfortable experience?
- Have you used alcohol to create more intimate experiences within relationships?
- Have you used alcohol to feel like you're more a part of a group, or like you can fit in more easily?
- Have you used alcohol to feel like you can simply be a normal human who's not so sensitive to everything going on around you— other people's feelings, worries, traumas?
- Have you ever used alcohol as a vacation from your everyday worries and burdensome weight you carry around?
- After a drinking period, have you ever felt particularly confused, like you've absorbed an intense emotional or physical experience that you didn't have in your system prior?

You may be reading this list and thinking that you identify with every single qualifier...or perhaps that none of these apply to you. Again, just consider with care and reflection what is most helpful for you, what you identify with, what can be used for your own ongoing inquiry and contemplation, and then take what you need and leave the rest.

WHY ALCOHOL CAN BE ESPECIALLY PROBLEMATIC FOR EMPATHS

If you are an empath and identify with some of the definitions and tendencies shared thus far, I invite you to think about building an entirely new framework of self-leadership and responsibility. This might sound daunting, but it's really just another way to practice self-care. When you become a student in mastering your emotional, spiritual, and energetic experience, you will immediately tune into how alcohol and other mind-altering substances and escapisms aren't going to serve your optimal well-being. For empaths, clarity and groundedness in your own being—two things alcohol robs you of—are paramount to living a happy, fulfilling life.

You may find that intimacy and creating genuine, deep connections in your relationships is incredibly challenging. Perhaps using alcohol and other substances along the way has helped you socialize more easily. Perhaps alcohol has helped you to experience life as a normal person to some extent, by numbing out your intensity and making sense of the world in which you find yourself. What would it be like to release that crutch now and forever in exchange for knowing (and loving) yourself more deeply? What would it be like to face your fears and confront your resistance head on, to identify the root of your challenges and ultimately set yourself free?

It's up to you. You always have a choice. And the beautiful part of the empowered empath journey is you get to be your own most powerful guide, the leader of your most extraordinary life. You decide: what feels best for you? What would it be like to let go of a crutch you've been leaning on, even if just for a week or a month to see how it feels?

At the end of the day, if you're not growing (emotionally, spiritually, physically, mentally), what are you actually doing? Staying still? We are designed to grow and expand as the powerful beings that we truly are. How are you challenging yourself to grow outside of your comfort zone and truly step into your embodied power?

BE GENTLE WITH YOURSELF

There are days when it can feel incredibly heavy and seemingly impossible just to be—to be a human, never mind an empath. In the past I used to check out (using alcohol and other substances) to avoid feeling whatever was coming up and wanting to be released. While it may have seemed to mute my senses and prevent me from experiencing the apparent pain and dis-ease I felt subject to, alcohol and drugs actually heightened these sensations. My alcohol consumption also ultimately created a deep sense of repression of everything I was feeling, so the looming discomfort not only continued but worsened over time.

One of the biggest transformations I've experienced and continue to experience in my journey as an empowered, empathic soul who has abstained from alcohol for a number of years is to take it easy on myself, celebrate how far I've come, and have a high degree of compassion for how challenging my experience can be at times. A commitment to practicing sacred rituals of grounding, celebration, clearing, and gratitude has been essential to my continuous growth and integration.

EMPATHS AT WORK

You could say it has become a part of our cultural conditioning to use alcohol as a self-medicating treatment for stress and overwhelm, regardless of whether or not the actual byproduct of drinking delivers the desired result of peace and ease. And what do you think tends to be one of the other leading causes of stress, especially in the Western world?

Work, of course. If you're awakening to your empathic nature, chances are you've felt your sensitivity particularly activated in work settings involving close work and collaboration within a group.

Regardless of whether you're working in a full-time job and putting in at least forty hours a week or an entrepreneur who's visiting all sorts of different work environments, interacting with different kinds of people all day, it's crucial to prioritize taking care of yourself during those long days. Exactly how you do that will depend a lot on your specific situation, but take time to consider your work environment, the dynamics and interactions in which you typically find yourself operating, and the personalities you encounter on a daily basis. Then it's time to brainstorm and create your own unique measures to ensure that your environment—particularly if you're spending the majority of your waking hours in a certain place—is nourishing your mind, body, and soul accordingly.

Here are some ideas to get you started:

- Place a Himalayan salt lamp on your desk to absorb electronic waves and emit a cleansing energy into your immediate atmosphere. This specific type of salt is known to absorb contaminated particles from the air while also taking positive ions out of your immediate environment, creating an instantly clearing effect. (It may be surprising to hear, but in this case you actually want more negative ions around, even though that sounds backward!) When heated up, the salt lamp releases the cleansed water vapor back into the air while also expelling negative ions that help activate ciliary activity in your lungs, improving your capacity to breathe and experience a clear flow of oxygen. Salt lamps are particularly helpful if you have respiratory issues and can also support you in enjoying a more positive mood and better sleep (both by-products of breathing more deeply and clearly).
- If you work inside, take frequent walks outside to get fresh air, move your body, and check in with yourself about how you are feeling.

- Use very direct communication with your coworkers, your boss, or even clients to establish healthy boundaries regarding what you are available for and when (and what you are unavailable for).
- Identify colleagues at your job who you feel most nourished by and make a point to invite them to spend more time with you, whether as friends or as mentors.
- Identify people who leave you feeling drained or tired, and consciously make an effort to avoid interacting with them unless absolutely necessary. And whenever you do have to interact with such people, make a point to increase your self-awareness and don't allow them to affect your energy. You can do this by focusing again and again on these questions: how am I feeling? What do I need in this moment to take care of myself? What would feel good to do or say?
- Intentionally nourish yourself with healthy food throughout the day.

Just as you created rituals at home, you might want to ask yourself whether doing the same kinds of practices at work—your own work rituals throughout the day—might be helpful as well. Remember that you can work hard and be devoted to your job and still treat yourself as the absolute most important person in your life.

TECHNOLOGY DETOX

Hand-in-hand with your work life goes technology. But no, I'm not going to suggest you quit *Facebook*, get rid of your cell phone, and stop using email. However, just like you're becoming more conscious of how you're nourishing your body with food, people, places, and activities, you'll also want to take special care to detoxify the technological environment and digital spaces you occupy.

Just like you are making a commitment to establishing healthy boundaries in all your relationships, in how you spend your time, and where you focus your energy, it is important to do the same with your involvement in all digital communication, especially when it comes to social media. If someone's presence online feels draining to you, why expose yourself to it? Would you want to be around that person in real life? Of course not, so why interact with someone like that online?

WHY A TECHNOLOGY DETOX IS ESPECIALLY IMPORTANT FOR EMPATHS

Technology and social media can be challenging channels for anyone to manage, let alone an empath. There's such an intense array of overstimulation available to everyone in every moment—in addition to all the extra energetic information you're already receiving via your amplified sensitivity. But you may find that as you prioritize what truly makes you feel good, your desire to constantly check your feeds fades away. The more you commit to being present and at peace with yourself in this moment, especially tuning into your body and the magic it is always sharing with you, you may find that you become increasingly disinterested in the distractions offered by the digital world. As you crave more intimacy and depth in your relationships due to the deepened love you cultivate for yourself, you'll find that real connection is the ultimate gift you're designed to experience. You'll likely want to create more opportunities in your life to experience precisely that, and a lot more often. Plus, while social media can do a great job connecting us on a certain level, it's no substitute for actually *living* your life.

TIPS FOR MINDFUL TECHNOLOGY USE

Energy speaks volumes, and as an empath, you're taking it all in— even if it's through a computer or a phone screen as opposed to in person. Take responsibility for your energy and how the energy of others affects you. Unfollow, disengage, clear your space of anything and anyone that doesn't completely nourish you in the ways you deserve to feel supported, loved, and empowered. If it's hard to do so, ask yourself why that may be. And again, people who trigger you are in your life to teach you lessons and catalyze your next-level freedom and growth. Always be curious as to what your triggers, especially on social media, may have to teach you along your empowered evolutionary path.

Here are a few ways to approach this task that you might find helpful and supportive along your empath journey:

- Limit social media use to one hour per day maximum. If you can take longer breaks, perhaps even an entire day, all the better. Give your soul breathing room to be in your own body, free from the overstimulating experience that is the vortex of the Internet and social media in particular.

- Pay attention to what energy you're exposing yourself to on your social media channels. Cleanse your space and start treating every element of information you expose yourself to with heightened intentionality. You deserve to feel supported, and your energy is precious. Take care of YOU first. Just like in real life, ask yourself the same questions you would regarding relationships in your life that you may be ready to let go of:

  - Are you feeling drained by any particular content or people in your digital world?

  - What would it be like to unfollow or unfriend anyone who's exuding a negative or draining energy that's not supporting you?

- Be mindful of how much time you spend looking at your phone, getting sucked into Internet surfing, or reading mindless articles. Try to limit phone use overall and instead make sure you're intentionally carving out space for creative time with just YOU, or with friends in real life doing what you love to do. Social media and the Internet can feel like a substitute for the interaction that you deeply desire, but remember that what you really crave is probably soulful, intimate connection with yourself and others...and most often, that's done in person.

- Be mindful of the types of media content you expose yourself to, especially if you're notoriously sensitive to sad, violent, scary, or any other intense story lines that upset your peace of mind. Just like you feel other people's negative energy, watching hours of fear-based news or horribly depressing documentaries or anything in that vein can have a similarly harmful effect on you. It can all feel so real, almost like it's happening to you.

- If you do elect to consume content that feels energetically intense to you, be sure to keep coming back to yourself throughout your viewing experience so you are sure to not lose yourself too much in the content. Periodically stop what you are watching to ask yourself: how am I feeling? Do I need anything in this moment to feel supported? Would anything else make me feel more comfortable? Then simply give that to yourself, whatever it is you need in that moment. Don't wait.

CREATE DAILY RITUALS

Cultivating a beautiful, loving relationship with yourself is central to living a fully empowered existence. Creating your own sacred, grounding rituals will ensure that you are nourishing your mind, body, and soul on a daily basis. Allow your daily rituals to be your most sacred time of every day. Make time and space to celebrate the gift that you are and to cultivate strength in the precise ways you desire so you can live the most fulfilled, vibrant life possible. Mindful rituals that help connect the mind, body, and soul are especially important for empaths.

Something that was powerfully infused into my consciousness during a lengthy stay I had in Bali was the notion that life truly is a ceremony. The reverence and respect I witnessed in the Balinese cultural practices of making offerings, adorning the streets with special décor, and donning sacred temple attire for multiple occasions each week was breathtaking. As I observed the local Balinese place offerings in front of every home each morning, I realized that there is absolutely so much to be grateful for, most of which we can't physically see but can feel when we tune in at a deeper level. Life certainly is a ceremony peppered with moments that are reserved for all of our sacred rituals.

When you think about it, aren't you already practicing rituals anyway? You probably have a morning routine or a special way you get ready for bed. Now is the time to get intentional about how you are practicing so that you are diverting your energy only to the outlets that feel most nourishing and supportive for your soul. Consider the habits presently appearing in your life, such as the way you walk to particular destinations, the familiar routes you take, the way you prepare food, the way you have conversations, the way you wake up in the morning, the way and times in which you exercise, etc. Again, life is a ceremony filled with a series of rituals, but not all of them—and in fact very few of them—are conscious. What would it be like to make every habit you are engaged in fully intentional?

STARTING NEW RITUALS

You may be wondering where you can start. One starting point, as with most other new commitments you'll be creating along your empath empowerment journey, is to be very clear about how you want to feel first and foremost. You can ask yourself how you want to feel in meditation or via journaling, or even in a conversation with someone you would love to be accountable to in developing your new commitments. What do you intend to receive as a result of your newfound commitment? Once you have a clear semblance of how you want to feel, you can get creative with what feels most aligned to support you in embodying your desired states. For example, if you want to feel more clearly focused and energized, you might start a daily ritual of doing a grounded meditation, followed by an energizing breathwork practice (breath of fire is a classic!) to create space for expansion in your body and life. Or, if you want to feel calmer and more at peace, consider trying a sound healing meditation perhaps utilizing Tibetan singing bowls, tuning forks, or a gong, alongside aromatherapy with oils that soothe your soul. You have an entire blank canvas to work with—how exciting! What are you adding to it? What colors will you use? How will your rituals support you? You decide.

One of my favorite rituals to guide people in creating is a before-bed practice that supports the cultivation of deep relaxation, intentionality around your dreams, and even sets into motion subconscious reprogramming while you sleep. Results from integrating this ritual on a regular basis could include improved sleep quality, more vivid dreaming with similarly vivid recall, more energy upon waking, and an overall strengthened sense of grounding in your own intuition and innate healing power. This ritual entails the following steps. Feel free to follow them as listed to see how it feels and then add or subtract whatever elements feel more or less in alignment with your supernatural flow:

1. Decide on what time you'd like to start getting ready for bed so you start programming your body to relax and begin your wind-down process with plenty of time to settle in. Typically, I suggest you start winding down from all technology, work, and DOING in general at least three hours before you plan on sleeping.

2. If you don't have one already, create a sacred space that you know can be your wind-down ritual area from now on. This can be an altar where you meditate and/or pray. It can be a cozy part of your house such as your couch or your favorite chair. It can be wherever you want—but the more consistently you claim one particular space as your wind-down area, the more easily you will feel the effects this ritual offers. Your body will start to recognize the cues you're setting up for it as soon as you land in your special space, so after a while your new program gets set into motion almost too easily.

3. Create a nourishing ritual with a drink that soothes your soul—such as a hot tea, an herbal tincture, or some other kind of relaxing potion that you really love. It can feel like a celebration—a treat for you that you come to look forward to as your wind-down nourishment. Chamomile with lemon, passion fruit, hibiscus, or any other kind of herbal tea you like may do the trick. I personally love creating special concoctions with different herbal blends and various adaptogenic blends with healing properties, such as cacao, reishi, and ashwagandha. (Disclaimer: for many people cacao is energizing, so it might not be the best thing for you to try before bed if you are sensitive. I, however, find it really relaxing to sip on in the evening a few hours before bed.)

4. Infuse whatever concoction you create with the healing intentions you'd like to bring with you in dream time. Is there anything you'd like to have resolved in your dreams? Any states you'd like to embody in your dreams? Any answers you'd like to receive?

5. In your sacred space, journal on your day: what are you celebrating about YOU today? What are you most proud of? What did you create that you're feeling deserves acknowledgment? What are you grateful for? What, if anything, came up as a challenge that you are growing through? Empty your mind here so you can clear your consciousness of any thought loops. Journal your intentions for dream time.

6. Listen to a sound healing meditation or use your own sound healing instruments such as singing bowls, tuning forks, a gong, or anything else that feels soothing for you to receive healing energy from before bed. Binaural beats programmed to certain targeted frequencies are incredibly powerful tools for integrating new subconscious programs depending on what your intentions may be. *YouTube* is a great reference for this kind of free content. See what feels best for you.

7. Once you're in bed, ensure your technology isn't just powered down but that it's also far away from arm's reach so you're not tempted to

pull yourself out of your deeply relaxed state. On that note, can you afford to set a boundary time-wise for when you consciously use your technology? What would it be like to set a time that you first pick up your phone each day and likewise when you power down completely? Where can you add more conscious intentionality to your technology use? What if using your phone and computer became more like your daily rituals in and of themselves? You decide.

The beautiful thing about your daily rituals is that they are all your own. You can create whatever you want, however you want—you make the rules. You may find it inspiring to try many different possible approaches and create your own practice from all of your varied experiences, or you may find that one simple practice works perfectly for you. Another consideration to keep in mind is timing. Once you are clear on how you desire to feel, is time of day important to factor into your equation? Do you find that you need more support and a deepened connection in the morning, afternoon, or evening, or all of the above and throughout your day? Tune in and ask yourself what feels most supportive, and then give yourself the gift of practicing precisely what feels best for you.

Here are some daily ritual ideas to further inspire you:

- MEDITATION: Any type of meditation practice that gets you into your body, into your heart, and tapped into your intuitive wisdom (which we'll talk more about later) is perfect. The more grounding the better, and preferably practiced first thing in the morning to set the tone for your day ahead.

- BREATHWORK: Deep breathing for a few minutes on a repetitive cycle can be immensely helpful. You could also consider a guided practice to elevate your consciousness, clear away stagnating energy, and open your heart. A powerful yet simple practice to try is the box-breath method in which you inhale for four counts, hold for four counts, exhale over four counts, and stay empty on your exhale for four counts. Alter this pattern as you see fit—extending or shortening your count. You know what feels best for you.

- SOUND HEALING: Whether you have your own crystal bowls, Tibetan bowls, a gong, a rattle, a rain stick, a drum, or tuning forks—or any other instruments you find to be immensely healing—spend some time playing the music that helps you feel supported, inspired, cleared, and connected.

- MOVEMENT: Move in a way that feels good, but make sure you commit to moving every day—whether it's light stretching, yoga, or more rigorous dance or cardio. Listen to your body and move how it wants to move.

- SELF-MASSAGE: When was the last time you luxuriated in massaging yourself with beautiful oil? This is a powerful grounding practice that also activates your pleasure centers to amplify your ability to receive clear guidance from your intuition. Plus, it simply feels amazing. Talk about treating yourself like someone you love!

- JOURNALING: Dedicating space for stream of consciousness writing is a transformative tool for connecting to your inner wisdom and emptying your mind of any to-dos, stories, or anything else on repeat that might be distracting you from your deeper truth. You can journal in response to a question you may have and allow your intuition to answer, or journal simply to empty your mind.

- AROMATHERAPY: Tune into which essential oils feel most nourishing for you. Do you have a favorite scent? How do certain oils make you feel? Try burning incense and candles to stimulate your senses as well as smudging with sage or palo santo to cleanse energy in yourself as well as within your space.

- EARTHING: Getting out into nature and putting your feet into the ground is a healing practice called earthing that will be especially beneficial for empaths who feel more comfortable existing in an ethereal, airy state. The more you can ground into nature and take deep breaths to really soak in the effects, the better.

- GRATITUDE: Try writing a gratitude list every day, listing the things you are celebrating about yourself, your life, and your vision. The more you can focus gratitude on yourself for the things that are special about you, the more you will notice a shift in your self-worth and self-esteem.

- CONNECTION: Does it feel nourishing for you to connect with loved ones more consistently? Consider how integrating this practice into your daily life might feel nourishing to you if more intimate, loving connection is something you desire.

- DIVINATION: An incredible tool for playing with and strengthening your intuitive guidance system is to work with oracle cards or other divination tools. There are infinite types of decks out there to choose from, and the fun part is picking one that you resonate with most deeply. Never heard of oracle cards before? Do a little research and see if you feel aligned with exploring this tool more intentionally. Other divination tools might include pendulums, crystals, shells, and the *I Ching*.

- ART: Making art, such as a vision board, is a fantastic way to connect to your intuition and your soul-self. Do you enjoy expressing yourself creatively? Which way feels best? Experiment and give yourself time and space each day to create whatever wants to come through you.

When it comes to daily rituals, there really are endless options for you to play with. What's most important above all else is to cultivate a daily practice that you look forward to, something that can be your rock in your daily life no matter what to anchor you into your present, embodied experience. Remember, you make the rules. Your only barometer for success is how good you feel. How exciting is it to look at life as a beautiful, continuous ceremony made up of rituals—that you get to create based on what feels most empowering, celebratory, and abundant for YOU? I love the idea of living in a world in which everyone is consciously choosing to create their lives based on their most powerful, activating practices to infuse more love, joy, and fun into our collective everyday experiences.

UPGRADING CURRENT RITUALS

If you already have your daily practices going strong, perhaps it's time for an upgrade. Ask yourself:

- Do I look forward to my practice and rituals?
- Do I feel inspired by them?
- Do they help me feel nourished and fulfilled?
- If your rituals aren't quite helping you feel how you want to feel, what can you do to change them so they do?

These are some helpful starting points to get clear on how you can give yourself precisely what your soul is requiring to feel totally empowered. As always, trust that you have the best answers for yourself.

CREATING A SPECIAL SPACE FOR YOUR RITUALS

One thing that can complement your ritual practices of self-care and nourishment is having a sacred space in which to do some or all of them. Do you have a space for your meditation practice, for your sacred or cherished objects? Consider creating one if you don't have it already, or upgrading if you have one that could use a little more life. Even just your own corner or nook will do. How can you create a space that feels nurturing and inspiring—like somewhere you can't wait to be every day? Have fun creating precisely what you envision and watch how powerful you'll feel tuning into your space each day as a source of deep connection and grounding within your being.

RITUALS BECOME ONGOING SUPPORT SYSTEMS

I didn't get into the practice of creating my own daily rituals until I got sober and was invited to do things I had never done before as part of my regimen and reprogramming for recovery. I felt like I was starting life over and as such learning to live from square one, learning how to be a human in many senses. Part of my initial daily program as far as my rituals were concerned involved prayer, meditation, journaling, and making phone calls to people I cared about. At the time, what I really desired was to feel free of the fear that had been dominating my life for so long, as well as a connection to a higher power outside of me that I could trust to take care of me. I didn't want to worry so much and I didn't want to feel like I had to be in control of everything, as I had felt for so long.

My rituals helped support me in anchoring in those precise states of being, and with continued practice they became more and more my default responses to how I took care of myself when challenging moments would arise. That's the other thing about daily rituals: when practiced consistently, you are actually building new "muscle memory" that will serve you powerfully in times when you most need support.

My commitment to my daily practice really was similar to going to the gym and lifting weights, but instead of building new muscles, I was building emotional and spiritual strength for the moments in life in which extra energy and clarity was required of me. Also, just like your physical workout probably changes and evolves as you get stronger or faster, your daily rituals will also naturally grow and evolve. It's important to constantly check in and stay inspired to give yourself the nourishment and support that you truly want.

DETOXING LIMITING BELIEFS

A limiting belief is something you believe to be true about yourself or your situation that is actually holding you back from living an authentic, abundant life. Most of us cultivate these limiting beliefs subconsciously as we grow up based on what we learn from our parents and our childhood environment. Even if you have a happy childhood and loving parents, limiting beliefs can creep in from other areas, especially from the societal pressures that tell you to act or look a certain way. Some common self-limiting belief are:

- I'm not enough as I am.
- There's something outside of me that will complete me.
- I'm not lovable.
- I'm not worthy of being supported.
- I'm not important.
- I am not capable of taking care of myself in the ways I truly need.

For empaths, self-limiting beliefs tend to be particularly centered on unworthiness—feeling unworthy of love and success, and feeling inhibited from being fully powerful—as well as an inherent lack of trust in themselves and the universe to provide the right support. In my case these limiting beliefs arose as a result of learning from an early age to focus more on my outside appearance than my internal, intuitively guided experience. I learned to believe that what people thought about me defined my value. I learned that how I looked mattered more than how I felt. This learning was instilled in me from a combination of early family conditioning as well as societal programming at large. As far as my family is concerned, I learned that I could wrest an appreciative reaction from my parents as long as I appeared successful, particularly in school. Actually, this belief goes even deeper. I'll share the story that I uncovered just a few years ago that unearthed a lifelong pattern for me in which I had been living for everyone else, always trying to look good instead of feeling good and hence living in a very confused state for quite a while.

In an early meditation I was seeking to meet my inner child to uncover the first memory in which I felt abandoned or like I didn't receive the love I needed from my caretakers. I sensed there was ripe insight to uncover here that would help me free myself of the longtime pattern I had developed to constantly determine my value based on what others thought of me instead of how I saw myself. Now, first things first: the intention of sharing this isn't to berate my parents whatsoever. They really are the most perfect parents I could have possibly chosen. Instead my intention is to show how subconscious programs can get set into motion early on simply by illustrating how I unconsciously created a story about myself that was instigated by an underlying uncomfortable, scary feeling of aloneness.

The memory I identified happened around age five when I was excited about watching a movie with my dad and my little brother. My mom was the only one we were missing, so I tried to rally her to join us. I remember knocking on her office door and asking her to join us, but she said something to the effect of "not right now"—which instead of simply accepting I took to mean something completely different. I took her response to mean something about me personally—that only if I was more impressive, that if I looked better, that if I was more important to her, then maybe she would come join us for the movie and I could feel like I had the connection between my family that I always desired. In that moment I programmed into my consciousness the story that would go on to guide me for years to follow, which essentially said: the better I look, the more impressive I am, the more successful I am, the more important I am, the more I am worthy of being loved. Really this can be boiled down even further to: if I am successful, I am important, and therefore I am loved. At the end of the day I was deathly terrified of being alone, so I learned to do anything at whatever cost to ensure I could always have the attention and affection of my loved ones to remind me of my value.

YOUR LIMITING BELIEFS CAN ACTUALLY GUIDE YOU TO YOUR GIFTS

As you become more energetically aware of your emotions, you'll start to see limiting beliefs and fears you have within you that are operating at a deeper level beneath the surface insecurities you may know all too well. So how can you detoxify these limitations and fears as you notice them pop up?

Well, first trust that a lot of your fear, self-doubt, and other limitations based in unworthiness or a fear of being alone (which has been my predominant experience in freeing myself on this journey of empath empowerment) are there to teach you the perfect lessons you need to grow through in order to experience the life you truly deserve to live. It's quite possible that you have a fear of being alone because you are actually meant to find the deepest connection of all, which is with yourself. Or, you might have a limiting belief that you are unworthy of love unless you do certain things for other people (meaning that your value and lovability is determined by how others see you) because you are meant to experience pure, unconditional love, not just for yourself but for everyone else you come into contact with.

The path to detoxifying yourself of beliefs and limitations and fears, many of which may feel like core parts of your identity and operating system, is a process for sure, but it starts as soon as you intentionally begin putting yourself first and treating yourself like you're the most important person in your life. Trust that by simply taking the new actions you're committing to through this process, many of your limitations will already naturally fall away without you needing to do anything consciously to remove them.

ACTIONS THAT HELP YOU DISCONNECT FROM LIMITING BELIEFS

There are many ways to bring awareness to your limiting beliefs so you can begin to rewrite your story. Depending on what limiting beliefs you're seeking to overcome, you may want to work on them alone or in a group, and progress may not happen overnight, but every step you take will bring you closer to fully enjoying your life like you truly deserve. Consider the following possibilities to support yourself in releasing what no longer serves you:

- Working with mentors who can help you specifically with spiritual transformation, mindset, aligning with your passion and purpose, or any other focus area you desire support in.
- Attending twelve-step programs or other types of spiritual communities that support you in connecting more deeply to your higher power, your sense of self, and your soul.
- Participating in transformational retreats and immersive experiences that nourish you and teach you practices and tools you can take with you for life to deepen your intuition and align more clearly to your purpose.
- Joining meditation and/or healing communities that offer support and help you keep up with your healing practices, especially if doing so entails receiving actual healing treatments such as Reiki or other kinds of energy work.
- Expanding your spiritual knowledge through books, training, consuming conscious content, and attending conferences either online or in person. For more ideas on how to continue your expansion, refer to the Resources section at the end of this book.
- Training in energy healing and intuitive reading modalities. It's highly likely that you have an extraordinary capacity to channel your empath gifts into healing; your invitation is to find the expression that feels best for you, which often starts with finding a modality that works well for you to heal yourself.
- Traveling is one of the most expansive ways to get to know yourself, develop strengthened self-trust, and see new perspectives that challenge your conditioning, and it often catalyzes deep transformation simply by helping you to see yourself in a new light.

Wherever you are in your path to detoxify your limiting beliefs, trust you are right where you're supposed to be. You are not reading these words by mistake. You are on a perfect path, designed just for you—trust that everything is unfolding in divine timing and know that there is no rush. Beyond your fear, doubt, and limitation lies your greatest gifts, your boldest light, your most powerful wisdom.

RADICAL FORGIVENESS

What does forgiveness, radical forgiveness at that, have to do with the empath experience? Well, everything. Practicing radical forgiveness will clear old energy that you may have been holding onto for god knows how long. If you've been feeling everything and everyone your entire life and are just now waking up to that fact, it's more than likely that you have a lot of memories you're holding onto that are ready to be released through intentional forgiveness practice.

It sounds easy enough, right? You can just forgive everything and everyone who has ever wronged you. Boom. Done. Released. Free. Technically, it could be that simple…but realistically, there is more to the process, thanks to the power of emotions and the stubborn stronghold of long-held feelings.

UNCOVERING YOUR RESENTMENT

The first time I really delved deeply into forgiveness was in a twelve-step program for my recovery from substance abuse. As part of the process I was invited to do an intensive inventory of all the people, places, ideas, and institutions that I felt resentful toward. Believe me, the list was long—I filled entire journals over the weeks that I worked on the massive project. A lot of this legendary "fourth step" was the emotional and spiritual equivalent of picking open scabbed wounds I had been carrying around with me for my entire life (and, in some cases, from many other lifetimes, as I discovered later on in my journey toward empath empowerment).

EXERCISE: HOW TO RELEASE LIMITING BELIEFS

Here's a helpful exercise to get clear on what's underneath your limiting beliefs. Your limiting beliefs and fears that tend to repeat on loops are typically some of the most powerful blocks in your way of being able to fully listen and trust your intuition.

With improved awareness, you can change and release the old to welcome in the new, and make space to receive your unique guidance in service to your ultimate truth. This tool has been central to my growth and so instrumental in the breakthroughs I help guide others through.

1. When you have a block, fear, or limiting belief presenting itself to you, write it down. Try following this example as your format by first inserting what your fear or limiting belief is, and following through all the ensuing feelings that arise. Here's an example:

   - **CURRENT FEAR: I'M AFRAID TO SHARE WHAT I'M REALLY FEELING.** *(What is the next thought to follow?)* Then I'll feel awkward. Then my message isn't coming across articulately. Then I lose the opportunities I need to be successful in my business, such as connecting with new clients. Then I am not even running a business and I'm stuck in my head. Then I'm alone, and I'm not producing anything of value or worth. There's no point to life. *Underlying belief: I'm worthless. What I have to offer isn't valuable.*

   - **OLD ACTION: GIVING UP.** *(What other specific actions are entailed in this example of your old response?)* Taking things personally when I haven't gotten opportunities I want. Not taking any action in the direction of my vision. Not sharing my value, message, or vision. Creating roadblocks to action. Self-sabotaging. Withholding, not sharing my truth. Getting resentful when I don't communicate honestly and other people misunderstand me. Feeling disconnected from others as a result.

- **OLD RESULT: BEING STUCK.** *(Which results in what?)* Not taking action, avoiding doing the things I really want to do. Not getting what I want. Feeling like I lack value. Self-fulfilling prophecy based in fear.

2. Now that you've listed out your old ways of being, it's time to create your soul-aligned truth-filled NEW ways of being that fully support you. Here's your example based on the flow previously detailed:

- **NEW BELIEF (HOW YOU WOULD LIKE TO FEEL INSTEAD): I AM INTRINSICALLY VALUABLE.** What I have to offer is extremely helpful to the world. I am worthy of divine compensation.

- **NEW ACTIONS: I CONNECT WITH EVERYONE AROUND ME.** I influence people and inspire them to live in their full possibility, connect with their own vision, and live more fulfilled, inspired lives. I do this by communicating my message through various channels, authentically, and honestly expressing how I feel creatively. I express myself with confidence and honesty in all conversations, always honoring my truth. I receive love and guidance from many relationships in my life. I happily invest in myself to feel guided and supported and to keep the flow of abundance active in my life. I receive incredible acknowledgment from all the people I help and inspire on a regular basis.

- **NEW RESULTS: I AM IN LOVE WITH MY LIFE, WORK IS FUN, AND EVERYTHING IS IN THE FLOW.** My self-care routine is easy to focus on, especially in the morning because then the rest of my day is fun. I am divinely inspired. I am living my dreams. I am in full integrity with my purpose. I feel like I am in the flow of life. I am rested, relaxed, and energized all at once.

3. Now you see clearly your entire flow of the old beliefs—and on the flip side, the truth that is actually in alignment with what you desire. How do you feel? Are you ready to take on your new actions that support you in embodying your desired states of being and subsequent results? You're off. It's time to fly.

4. This process is really powerful if practiced with someone who can hold you accountable to upholding your new committed actions, such as a mentor, a coach, a friend, or some other kind of adviser in your life who can help with your continued transformation.

Trust me, this exercise works. There's no quicker path to transformation than really putting your full skin in the game and saying (even if you don't believe it at first): I AM WILLING TO CHANGE and here's how I'll commit to new actions aligned with my true desires.

I made an impossibly extensive list of all the people, places, and things (and even ideas) I could possibly think of that had wronged me in some way, because I was instructed to hold nothing back. At first I thought that this process would be enormously fulfilling, assuming that after I wrote it all down, I would share my long list of complaints with someone else who would sympathize with me and validate my self-pity and righteousness.

We become what we think about all day long.

—Ralph Waldo Emerson

I couldn't have been more wrong. Instead, I soon learned that the point of this prescriptive exercise was actually to take full responsibility for the ways in which I had "set the ball in motion" in each situation. For each person, idea, or institution I listed, after filling out the ways in which each element triggered me, I spent an equal part of the exercise investigating how I had catalyzed much of the misunderstanding and disagreement inherent in each situation, largely rooted in my attachment to the unrealistic expectations I had been holding everyone to. Through this process I finally became aware of my deepest subconscious patterns, which kept certain cycles of suffering in motion.

The final part of the extensive exercise was to fully own my part in the matter and see where I could let go of any attachment to being right or feeling validated. Where could I forgive myself and all other parties involved? It became clear to me that holding onto these old resentments and triggers, many of which had transpired years ago, was like me drinking poison and hoping other people would feel the negative effects. It was pure insanity. But most unconscious behaviors and patterns are like that, until they're finally illuminated and made conscious.

THE BENEFITS OF FORGIVENESS

If you resonate with the feeling of carrying burdens and an energetic heaviness around certain people, places, ideas, or institutions that trigger you or irritate you in some way, even if the trigger is rooted in a transgression from years ago, you will definitely benefit from a forgiveness practice. Use the following exercise to do an initial clearing of anything you may be holding onto, then utilize it again periodically to clear your energy field of anything you may have subconsciously absorbed.

Why does practicing forgiveness end up being an invigorating energetic tune-up for your sweet empathic soul? Because you get to be completely free of any and all attachments you're carrying, especially the subconscious agreements you've made to take care of others. What a relief that you no longer have to carry that weight. Imagine how energizing it feels to no longer have to manage all that sensory information you've been carrying around. You'll know what I mean as soon as you start experiencing the sweet spaciousness of truly letting go in the ways I describe.

In my case forgiveness became an ultimatum following my powerful realization of the truth: by holding onto past wrongs, disappointment from unfulfilled expectations, and anything else that was causing me anguish to any degree, I was the one suffering the most. And so it was forgiveness that was clearly my most powerful anecdote. For me, my process of letting go required facing uncomfortable truths regarding how I acted upon certain unconscious beliefs, and how my responses created all sorts of disruption in my life.

Going through the arduous process of witnessing my behavior patterns through writing an inventory was crucial in instigating my surrender. I could see that I had no choice but to forgive myself first and foremost for operating oftentimes in fear, underpinned with a strong desire to protect myself and feel safe. After I forgave myself for my own unjust behaviors, it was much easier to forgive all the other entities in my life who I had previously blamed for so much of my dis-ease.

EXERCISE: LETTING GO; YOUR ULTIMATE ENERGETIC TUNE-UP

The first time you do this exercise, dedicate an hour or more to it so you can excavate whatever comes up. (This could also be an ongoing project if your initial list is long.) (Note: this exercise is inspired by the fourth step from the twelve steps of Alcoholics Anonymous.)

1. Take some deeply relaxing breaths, centering yourself and preparing yourself to receive some truth about yourself. Tune into your heart and establish a feeling of being rooted to the earth beneath you. You are safe and protected as you seek to know the truth. You can even repeat this affirmative statement aloud as a mantra if it supports you: I am safe and protected as I seek to know the truth.

2. Grab your journal or a piece of paper and start listing the names of people, places, ideas, and institutions that have bothered you, irritated you, or triggered you in any way whatsoever.

3. Once your list is complete, next to each entity write what this entity did to cause you to feel irritated. Write as much as you need to feel fully expressed, but keep in mind simplicity is a great guideline.

4. Next to this, start a new column in which you write how each transgression impacted your sense of safety. Ask yourself the following questions: how did this situation make me feel unsafe? How did I give away my power?

5. Your final column is dedicated to taking back your power. Knowing that you can't change the past, how do you take care of yourself in this present moment to achieve true growth and acceptance? What could you have done differently to avoid the particularly triggering, irritating outcome? What do you now know to be true? What will you commit to doing (or *being*) differently going forward?

As an example, here's a sample row:

TRIGGER: I KEEP HAVING TO REMIND A FRIEND TO PAY ME BACK FOR THE LOAN I OFFERED HIM MONTHS AGO.

WHY IT BOTHERS ME.	HOW MY SAFETY/ SECURITY IS IMPACTED.	WHAT COULD I HAVE DONE DIFFERENTLY? WHAT CAN I DO DIFFERENTLY GOING FORWARD?
I don't like having to talk to friends about money	He might not respect me because he doesn't take me seriously enough to pay me back in time	I could have been more specific about when I expected to be paid back and had it confirmed in writing
I don't like to seem like I need money	He doesn't think I am important; maybe I'm not important	I could have explained that I would only loan the money if it was absolutely agreed that I would be paid back on a particular date
I want my friend to pay me back because it's the right thing to do	Maybe people don't take me seriously	I can make contracts for any future loans I make to people
I shouldn't have to ask for something so obvious	Maybe I don't deserve respect	I forgive myself and thank myself for learning this lesson: clarity in my financial relationships is extremely important to me and I will take care of myself in this realm going forward
I don't like to seem annoying or pestering	If I don't get my money back I will feel like my bank account is low	
I feel like if he respected me he would pay me back immediately; maybe he doesn't think highly of me	I might not trust other friends to take loans from me again, which could be a threat to my friendships	

This is an extensive process, but I promise if you do it with rigor and attentiveness you will experience immediate results—most notably an sense of spaciousness within you to receive love and connection. You will ultimately see that your triggers are your greatest teachers. You are responsible for how you respond and as such, you are completely empowered to free yourself of any heaviness or expectations that have been weighing you down or creating any blocks to receiving the love and connection you truly desire and deserve. You are completely empowered to activate your own freedom.

MANAGING YOUR EXPECTATIONS OF OTHERS

Just like we saw in the previous exercise around cultivating forgiveness for yourself and others by consciously observing your triggers and thanking them for the lessons they offer, managing your expectations of others offers similarly beneficial catalysts for your growth. As an empath, being aware of any tendency you have toward carrying resentment from false expectations or unfulfilled promises is crucial to your well-being. Consider how having unfair expectations of others could very well be the source of much of the anguish and exhaustion you are currently feeling or have experienced in the past. It's possible that your expectations of others, however perfectly reasonable they seemed at the time, could have been rooted in your pattern of seeing the best in people before they can really see themselves. If you have set expectations for people in your life to raise their standards and act accordingly, and they fail to do so, you may need to reassess your expectations and why you have them.

It could be that you're cultivating this cycle unknowingly. As an empath, it's easy to see the best in others and expect them to rise to the occasion to embody their highest possibility. And this is a beautiful gift you possess: to see the truth in others and see what they are truly capable of, almost as though you're able to tune into others at the soul level. This is precisely what is happening as you become more aware of your ability to tune into other's energy with greater discernment.

But like so many other burdens you've likely taken on as your own, expecting others to rise to the occasion repeatedly to embody their absolute best isn't only unrealistic but completely unfair to your well-being. Remember, your job now that you know who you are and why you're here is to take care of yourself no matter what, above all else. It's not your responsibility to make sure others experience fulfillment and embodiment of their highest possibility, believe it or not. And what a relief that you have no control over whether or not that happens. Regardless of any outcomes, you're perfectly fine as long as you're putting yourself first.

But what happens if you're feeling let down repeatedly by people, especially those whom you care about the most and who aren't living up to their full potential—which you can see as clear as day? First and foremost, recognize that you have the gift of sight, that part of your empath power is to feel what people, especially those closest to you, are truly capable of. You can see who they are, you can feel what they're really feeling, and you can see their truth sometimes before they can see it for themselves. Part of your lesson in discerning your own energy and sticking to your own lane is to recognize when you have expectations of others that aren't realistic and may in fact be causing you disappointment and impairing your ability to enjoy life. Herein lies an important lesson and opportunity to create healthy boundaries, which we'll go into even deeper in a later chapter.

How can you stop holding people to a certain standard if you keep finding yourself disappointed by their shortcomings? Well, you don't want to allow yourself to settle for less than what you deserve when it comes to quality relationships, but ultimately you get to decide what *quality* means for you in each and every case. Here's where you are being asked to be the radically honest, responsible leader of your own life. What is your standard for healthy relationships? What are your nonnegotiable needs when it comes to how you expect people to treat you (and surely how you agree to treat others as well)? You decide.

AMELIA'S EMPATH EXPERIENCE

Once I got sober and started to actually feel my emotions, I finally tuned into how much resentment I was carrying within my consciousness. There was so much I was holding against other people and myself that I had never been aware of until I started to finally feel all the pain I had been numbing with substances. I realized that I had learned to have very high expectations of others according to what would suit me best. This was a survival mechanism I developed to keep myself safe and maintain some semblance of control over my life.

The alternative would have been to trust that the universe was taking care of me, and know that I didn't need to take care of anyone else or even have expectations of them. My only job was to focus on me. But for most of my life this wasn't an option for me; it was too scary to be in this human experience all alone. My expectations ended up being my security blanket, really. As long as I could expect others to act a certain way, I knew what to plan for. But living like this only set me up for disappointment after disappointment, in a repetitive cycle that would take over two decades to fully play out.

Letting go of my need to control everything and release all forms of expectations and ultimately free myself of resentment helped me to make space for the love and connection I desired.

MEETING YOUR INNER CHILD

Remember who you were before you were taught to be someone else? When you believed in magic? When you had total faith that you were taken care of? When you were simply here to play and explore and have fun? Sound familiar? Have you interacted with this part of yourself since you were a child? If it's the first time you're even considering this possibility, are you open to getting to know a deeper part of you in a new way?

Everyone has an inner child inside. This energy can sometimes feel like your soul or higher self—whatever term most resonates with you is perfect. What comes up for you when you consider interacting with this part of you? Acknowledging your inner child and opening a dialogue with this part of you is an incredibly profound stepping stone on the path to self-love, healing, and a transformed relationship with trust. It's time to reconnect with your innate unshakable faith that you are always taken care of, and let the miracles begin to unfold.

Easier said than done, I know—but it's so important to try.

Intensity-seeking is an enslavement of our own perpetuation. When we step out of the delirium of always seeking someone new, and meet the same old sad and lonely child within, our healing journey begins. Exhausting ourselves with novelty is a defense against our deepest pain, one that we cannot outrun. But once we stop and feel our losses, we can begin our healing journey and be the authentic, joyous person we were born to be.

—Alexandra Katehakis, *Mirror of Intimacy: Daily Reflections on Emotional and Erotic Intelligence*

WHY CONNECTING WITH YOUR INNER CHILD IS SO IMPORTANT FOR EMPATHS

Inner-child work is incredibly transformative, and for empaths the invitation is especially powerful. Tuning into the innate inner wisdom and innocence stored within your inner child is the key to connecting more deeply and freely with your inherent soul essence to embody your highest truth.

At some level most disharmony, violence, and suffering present in the world is a result of hurt people hurting other people. But why does the vast majority seem to be hurting? Well, Freud said in 1915 that only 10 percent of our individual (and therefore collective) actions are carried out in consciousness, so that means 90 percent of our behavior is motivated from unconsciousness, powered by subconscious beliefs. How are subconscious beliefs typically programmed? Most often they are developed from birth to age three while learning various attachment strategies from our caretakers (usually, our parents).

A person who never learned to trust confuses intensity with intimacy, obsession with care, and control with security.
—John Bradshaw, *Homecoming: Reclaiming and Healing Your Inner Child*

You can see how complicated it gets when you're an adult blindly operating from a program that you adopted as a primary survival mechanism when you were three. Yet so many beings are operating from exactly this type of experience, unaware of the subconscious motivations powering their beliefs, thoughts, and actions.

As an empath, perhaps you identify with absorbing certain programs and belief systems from your parents, including ones that your parents might have inherited from their childhoods and respective lineages. In fact, you might now be aware that you've been holding certain beliefs and operating systems that don't really feel like yours at all. And chances are they're not yours to manage any longer.

What might some of these programs be? A few examples of commonly experienced programs include:

- I'm not safe to be who I am.
- I have to perform to be worthy of love.
- Life isn't meant to be easy.
- I don't deserve to feel taken care of.
- If I am too powerful, I will be alone.

At the root of these beliefs are core wounds that all humans fundamentally share to some extent: abandonment, rejection, shame, guilt, and fear.

These wounds are ultimately the primary fuel of the 90 percent subconscious behaviors, thoughts, and beliefs that culminate in massive disharmony and imbalance across multiple facets of our individual and collective existence.

She held herself until the sobs of the child inside subsided entirely.
I love you, she told herself. It will all be okay.
—H. Raven Rose, *Shadow Selves: Double Happiness*

You may find in your empathic healing journey that you've acquired various subconscious programs from the collective consciousness that aren't yours to begin with but have nonetheless ingrained various survival strategies and coping mechanisms in you that you are now ready to release.

Your inner child is your soul essence embodied and knows nothing but love, innocence, and pure wonder. It is your adult self who is carrying such extensive trauma from all the various conditioning you experienced to fit in, to be safe, to be understood, and to feel accepted. As an empath, you likely identify with all of this but to a much more powerful, in-depth degree—you are carrying not only your own core wounding and perhaps that of your family lineage as well, but also that of the entire collective. You've carried quite a burden, and now it's time to release it fully and reconnect to your deeper truth.

Healing your relationship with your inner child is a powerful start to building the foundations of an abundant life. You'll strengthen your self-esteem and self-love, which leads to a powerful ability to discern energetic boundaries and intuition.

JESSICA'S EMPATH EXPERIENCE

I was craving more depth in the personal development work I had been doing on my own. I needed support in deepening my experience and getting back on track, especially with my sense of worthiness, trust, and self-confidence. I had discovered some deep trauma blocks that I hadn't been able to access and it was starting to occur to me that a physical injury I had been dealing with was rooted in an underlying spiritual-energetic issue. I knew my next chapter of transformation was going to require an immersion-type experience within an intimate retreat with lots of individualized support.

In the numerous other transformational programs I've participated in, I had never been able to access my three-year-old self, which happened to be the age at which many of my biggest traumas originated. During the intensive group work I participated in over the course of the retreat immersion, I was able to access this precise point in my life in a way I never had before. Our guided meditations helped me connect to the voice within me that had so many answers and insights to share, and through the intuitive letter writing in which I allowed my inner child to write to my adult self, letting me know how I could take better care of the little me, I healed more deeply than I ever had. At last I was setting myself free from the fear, sadness, and hiding that had up until that point been running my life.

The real hidden gold I uncovered was a deeply rooted pattern of not speaking up for my truth—which resulted in physical trauma and various other injuries and hardships largely as a consequence of repressing my energy and storing it unnaturally in various parts of my body. Our bodies are so wise, and all along mine was signaling to me through my various injuries that something else was out of balance, something that I ultimately had the power to correct and literally heal myself in the process.

LEARNING TO LOVE YOUR INNER CHILD

I know that inner-child work can be difficult, believe me. I first learned about my inner child in a healing session soon after my first

Reiki experience. I was taken through a guided inner-child healing meditation in which I was asked to visualize my inner child. What's amazing is how it's become an instrumental piece to my own healing, and how I now use this precise kind of work as a foundation for supporting my clients. But the first time was heart-wrenching.

At the end of the visualization I was asked to look my inner child in the eyes and tell myself: I love you. The feeling of not being able to say "I love you" to myself was so heartbreaking. It was just me finally alone with myself and when all was said and done, I couldn't bring myself to do it, like my imagined embodiment of my adult self in my psyche just couldn't get the words out to this little-girl version of me. I couldn't even say I love you in my imagination: what was that about?

Let us liberate ourselves from any form of control. Let us focus at the inner drum, where the rhythm aligns with that of our heart. The measure of responsibility, equals to the need for evolution. Just listen, the inner child, let it whisper in your ear.
—Grigoris Deoudis

The feeling was akin to breaking my own heart. I realized in that moment that I had been the one all along who was keeping the love I truly desired from myself. I was so sad to feel this truth, but I knew it was an important milestone on my journey back to myself. My whole journey to living as an empowered empath has been a journey back to my own center, a journey back to the home I've always sought in all the outside people, places, and things—the home that's always been within me, which of course is the last place I looked.

The inner-child meditation experience catalyzed an entirely new inspiration within me to approach self-care with renewed fervor. I saw how the entire life ahead of me depended on my ability to courageously face the truth about myself and start giving myself the love I so desperately sought from everything and everyone around me. I saw that as long as I continued to look outside of myself for love, it would never be enough, it would never really fulfill the deeper need I experienced. The answer was in me, and I had to start there.

EXERCISE: LET YOUR INNER CHILD OUT TO PLAY

There are infinite ways to tune into your inner essence, your inner child, your soul, your higher self—whichever archetype you most identify with. Which method excites you most? Which feels most in flow for you? Go with that. And be open to adapting, as you will surely grow and transform extensively throughout these practices. As a reminder, take what you need and leave the rest—these practices are meant to be inspiration for you to create your own practices and rituals that work for you. Use your powerful intuition to feed into what is most supportive for you and stick with it!

Here are some suggestions for how to access your inner child. Feel free to customize and personalize these in order to best cultivate your relationship with your little you. What happens when you do? Oh, just increased self-love, deepened trust in your intuition, improved intimacy in your relationships, increased intensity in your sensory perception, and increased joy and creativity.

- **MEDITATION:** Once you've taken some relaxing deep breaths, bring to mind a vision of yourself as a young child. (Whatever age first comes to mind is perfect.) Picture yourself at this time, in your totally innocent, pure essence. This is your little you. Say hello. Does your little you have anything to say? Does your little you need help with anything? Is it easy to hear the little you or do you feel like it's going to take some time? See what kind of relationship you can develop in this visualization practice by spending time every day getting to know you on this deeper level.
- **AWARENESS:** Periodically throughout the day, simply bring to mind the picture you have of yourself as a small child—whatever comes to mind when you think of your own inner-child essence is perfect. Check in with this pure essence of innocence within you.

Ask this part of yourself: what does your inner child need? What do you want? How can you cultivate a dialogue with yourself and really check in on a recurring basis throughout your day? Can you picture yourself holding your own little hand as you're going about your day? What kinds of soothing words and assurances can you provide yourself with?

- **CREATIVITY:** Write a letter, paint, or draw a picture—even better if you do so with your nondominant hand, as this taps into your inner-child energy by using the emotional, imaginative centers of your brain instead of the logical aspect. Allow your inner child to express itself through your art by answering these questions: what does your inner child like to do? What does she enjoy experiencing? How can you give her what she wants? How can you play? How does your inner child want to be fully expressed?
- **PLAY:** What did you enjoy doing when you were little? Can you tap into that type of fun today, even if just for a few moments? How can you create more time and space in your life for wonder, joy, and creativity? Tune into how you were when you were little. What did you always want to do? What mattered to you most? What did you believe in? How can you give yourself space and attention to embody these things now?
- **RITUAL:** Create a sacred space or altar in your home where you can meditate every day. Put a picture or perhaps an item that reminds you of your childhood there. Tune into this memory each day and celebrate yourself for your divine innocence and beautiful soul essence. Ask yourself what you are celebrating about you. What is special about you? What are your unique gifts and ways of being that deserve to be acknowledged?
- **BUILDING TRUST:** If you haven't been paying attention to your inner child for quite a long time, you probably need to reestablish

trust with little you. A great way to start this process is to allow your inner child to write a letter to your adult self, indicating the ways in which trust has been broken and where your inner child needs to feel loved, acknowledged, and taken care of. Let your inner child express the sadness, fear, worry, and anything else that's coming up to be released in a letter to your adult self, who is now responsible for and accountable to taking amazing care of the little you. The next part of this is for your adult self to write a letter to your inner child declaring what you're committed to going forward and all the ways you'll show up and be depended upon to keep the little you safe, happy, and loved.

Have fun! This relationship is all yours. Create what you need. Start from where you are now and enjoy getting to know this part of you that's been waiting for you to connect more deeply. Take note of any questions, resistance, and inspiration—anything at all that comes up in this process. Keep track of these insights in your journal so you can check back on your progress as you heal. Trust that this is such powerful transformational work you are embarking on, creating such a solid foundation for self-love and beautiful expansion.

CHAPTER 4
Self-Care for Your Energy

Despite being motivated by loving, positive intentions to serve the world in a grand capacity, once my intuitive, empathic sensitivity kicked into overdrive upon entering into adolescence, all bets were off. The incredibly overwhelming experience of my extreme emotions—mine and everyone else's—was too much. At the time, without any knowledge of what I was dealing with or that my experience was actually extremely amplified and quite different from that of most of my friends, survival, which manifested as an undying question to fit in, became paramount.

Had I learned earlier on that my empath experience was actually quite different from everyone else's around me, had I received tools and training with which to become truly empowered in my gifts, and had I most of all learned that nothing was wrong with me, that I just had a special gift I needed to give special attention to, perhaps I wouldn't have had to go down such a difficult path. But then again, if all of that had happened, I wouldn't be writing this book now. I wouldn't be writing these words for the teenager or young adult or parents or friends of another empath who is similarly struggling with just living, not knowing that there's nothing wrong with them at all: they're just missing a few simple tools that will allow everything to radically shift once and for all.

In my case, because of the severe energy drain and feeling of intense exhaustion I experienced day in and day out as a result of being such an open, energetic presence and a continual magnet for people and situations who drained my energy to the depths of my being, I turned to alcohol and then other substances to intentionally check out and turn it all off. It was too hard at the time to cope otherwise. I didn't understand how other people seemed to go about life with such ease and carefree sensibility. For me, everything had become so intense, like the entirety of the collective human experience depended on my every move.

What a weight to carry. But carrying everyone else's emotions, fears, doubts, and sadness is the heaviest thing there is. It's even heavier when you have no idea you're carrying it all and all the meanwhile you think something must be wrong with you. Why can't you just get it together and be normal? Why is everything so amplified? Why is it a constant battle to explain yourself to others when you're upset and deal with the rampant dishonesty and lack of consideration you receive in return? Does anyone really understand you or how much you really care? And so my internal dialogue went on for about ten years, even into getting sober at age twenty-four. I still had a lot of entanglements and old behaviors to clear up in order to become truly sovereign in my own energy as a powerful, energetic being.

UNDERSTANDING PERSONAL ENERGY

Regardless of where you are on your current journey into your awakening and discovery of your empathic, intuitive gifts, it's time to get real about energy. Let's face it, everything is made of energy, period. Deepak Chopra challenges us to take personal ownership of our energetic selves through working in therapy or healing with our emotions (which equate to energy in motion). He reminds us: "Dealing with your own energy is the most effortless way to heal yourself, because you are going directly to the source. When a distorted energy pattern returns to normal, the problem disappears."

WEST VS. EAST

The amazing presence of energy all around us can be an unusual thing for Westerners to hear about because of how differently Western science speaks about energy compared to other philosophies from around the world. It's important to consider, however, how Western science (with all its intrinsic requirements for empirical evidence and data) is significantly lagging behind when it comes to acknowledging the importance of our individual energy and energetic states in determining our health, well-being, and really all other circumstances that we as human beings face throughout our lives.

The fact is that mostly all cultural traditions across Eastern and Western thought have shared a common belief in the role of energy as part of universal cosmology. Plus, let's face it, since the dawn of humankind—as far as history can tell and certainly beyond the time frame in which words were available to denote the written record—we've wondered again and again why we are here and what the whole point of this life must be. There has to be a point after all—perhaps even a divine design. Maybe you've heard from some of the thought leaders at the forefront of such explorations, including Carl Jung, Joseph Campbell, Wilhelm Reich (Reichian psychology), Alexander Lowen (bioenergetics), John Pierrakos (core energetics), Barbara Brennan (humanism), and Deepak Chopra (quantum medicine), to name a few.

As our collective awakening continues to accelerate, it's becoming more commonplace to hear about energy as well as various energetic concepts being mentioned in the media, popular culture, and so on. How exciting is it to consider the ways in which you might be an invitation for others to join in the conversation in a more meaningful way simply by your mere energetic presence? The more clearly you understand how to manage your own energy, the more you can support others in becoming more energetically sovereign in their own right too.

If you want to find the secrets of the universe, think in terms of energy, frequency and vibration.

—Nikola Tesla

While the West may be slow in coming to terms with energy as the basis for our entire existence and subsequent multiple dimensions of our lives, Eastern spiritual and cultural traditions have indicated a reverence for the energy body and energetic interactions and impacts for a very long time. For at least thousands of years, studies and teachings on the energy body have been extensive focal points throughout Indian yogic philosophy, Tibetan Buddhism, and Chinese medicine, to name a few. According to the Energetics Institute, "This system broadly speaks to us of a system of energy flow from head to toe, with entry/exit points at both ends, and intermediate points of intake (charge) or discharge, principally along the spine as chakras (wheels of energy)...but also flowing lines/channels/meridians which navigate the body and impact organs and processes of the physical, mental and emotional self." Tuning into these systematic contexts is helpful for creating your own deeper understanding of how your own energetic body functions, flows, and interacts with the world around you. As with many other concepts shared in this book, awareness of your own energy is the first step in becoming fully empowered in your gifts.

MEDITATE, THEN MEDITATE MORE

One of the best things you can do for yourself as an energetically sensitive being is to meditate, meditate, meditate. Start getting in touch with yourself and connect to your idea of a higher power, your spiritual guides, and a belief system that feels most aligned with you. If you've never meditated before, you might think of it as just a time to sit in silence. But those quiet moments with yourself are your time to refuel and nourish yourself from a day that's likely filled with a lot of giving to others. The best way you can help anyone else is to first take care of you and make sure you feel incredibly nourished, so what better practice to commit to than daily meditation?

ADDRESSING MEDITATION MYTHS

First things first. Do you have any old beliefs or associations that come up when you hear the term *meditation*? Does it bring up anything for you? Do you have an idea of how "it's supposed to be" that perhaps feels rather daunting? In my experience many people don't meditate because they feel like they're not doing it right, or perhaps they try it once but feel like "it didn't work." There are so many sensationalized images and conceptions of what meditation is that have been conditioned into our collective consciousness—especially when it comes to "how it should look" and "how it should be." Unfortunately, many of these end up being more deterring than motivating when it comes to actually getting inspired to start a practice.

Let's clear this up immediately. According to Yoga International, meditation is simply the practice of "resting the mind and attaining a state of consciousness that is totally different from the normal waking state. It is the means for fathoming all the levels of ourselves and finally experiencing the center of consciousness within. Meditation is not a part of any religion; it is a science, which means that the process of meditation follows a particular order, has definite principles, and produces results that can be verified."

And what exactly does that mean? It means that meditation is a practice—a scientific one at that—that you can develop however feels best for you in order to experience a deep sense of connection with your intuition and soul-centered guidance. Meditation is like taking a vacation away from the part of your mind that's constantly flooding you with ideas and a nonstop flow of content to entertain, question, and sort through. How nice is it to tune out from the chatter and tune into a deeper peace within? Sweet relief.

We don't see things as they are; we see them as we are.

—Unknown

You may be thinking: *yes, that all sounds great, but how do I get to that place of enjoying peace within?* Perhaps you started to meditate and found that your mental chatter was so loud you could barely even focus long enough to listen to a guided meditation for a few minutes. I've been there—trust me. I first got into meditation after I got sober and really had no other choice but to accept spiritual help and guidance on how I could learn to actually be some kind of semblance of an actual human. (A decade of heavy drinking and escapism will do that to you.) All those years of intense partying during my formative adolescence and early adulthood stunted my emotional maturity to a huge degree—I didn't know how to interact with people in a genuine, intimate way or how to be alone with myself at all. I really did have to learn from scratch; I was re-creating myself on a brand-new foundation. Meditation was and continues to be one of my most essential tools in establishing my sense of truth while being grounded in my soul.

Eventually, meditating will become as happenstance as brushing your teeth in the morning. Enough practice consistently will anchor it into your habits just like that. And if you think about it, how much sense does that really make: we take showers to keep our physical bodies clean, but how about our energetic, spiritual bodies? Meditation is like a shower for your soul in just that same sense. Get used to regularly checking in on and upgrading your spiritual hygiene. I promise you'll experience immediate relief and quite likely incredible, expansive results both internally and externally.

CONSIDER JOINING A GROUP

When I first started meditating, I learned in groups. I found that going to a supportive community in New York City helped me to focus and really feel safe to practice what otherwise felt scary to do on my own. If I practiced alone, at times I would feel overwhelmed and like my mind was too loud to manage. Something about being in a group with other meditators around me was enormously helpful. I felt energetically supported by the group's dedication to creating a more peaceful existence, not only individually but collectively. I fed off this peaceful energy and received a major kick-start into my own practice simply by being around so many other dedicated meditators similarly seeking to quiet their minds and tune into their hearts.

If you're wondering where to find a group, an easy way to start is to simply research meditation groups around your local area. See what comes up and be open to trying a few options to find what feels best for you. We are also so fortunate to live in a time in which abundant resources for meditation and supportive communities are boundless. You can find numerous options for online communities, mobile apps, guided meditations, and other teachers that have their own communities in which you can find classes, personalized mentoring, and more. A few of my favorite tools for meditation to this end are:

- **Insight Timer**, which offers tons of guided meditations, including a fun social feature where you can see who else from around the world is meditating with you.
- **Inscape**, which hosts an in-person meditation studio in New York City as well as a dedicated app for guided meditations.
- **Journey Meditation** and **Deep Mindfulness Collective**, which offer tons of guided content on *YouTube* as well as individualized meditation mentoring.
- The book *Dharma Punx* by **Noah Levine** and **Against the Stream Buddhist Meditation Society** are other fantastic resources to check out, especially if you're interested in learning about meditation retreats and a diverse array of teachers around the world.
- The guided meditations on **my** *YouTube* **channel** as well as on my *Visionary Souls* **podcast**.

Have fun exploring all the different tools available to you and see what feels best. Follow your best feelings and let your intuition guide your way.

LEARN SOME TECHNIQUES

Learning general meditation techniques might also be helpful as you begin a meditation practice. Meditation isn't just about following your breath and watching it go in and out or "letting your thoughts go." I remember hearing someone instruct that in a class one time and thinking, but how? How do you let your thoughts go? I had no reference point for that even being possible, but I knew it was something I desperately wanted to experience. My thoughts were like a prison at times because some of the ongoing stories I told myself were so hurtful and negative. So I became curious about different techniques that could help me focus on new ways of using my energy to create different experiences and ultimately different results. I learned about ways to meditate that felt energizing and uplifting, ways that felt relaxing and made me tired, ways that felt like unplugging from my thoughts altogether, ways that felt elevating by focusing heavily on a particular sequence of breathing, and more. Everyone is different, so you'll learn what works for you.

Above all else, I've learned that meditation can actually be anything you want. You can walk, dance, sing, talk, hug, clean your house, organize your dishes, make art—anything you can imagine can be made into a meditation. The inherent qualifier is simply to do whatever it is you are doing mindfully, meaning:

- With patience
- Paying close attention to your breath
- Being as present as possible in your body throughout the experience

Nowadays, dancing is one of my favorite "moving meditations" because it really gets me into my body in a powerful way, allowing me to breathe deeply and tune into my present desires and expressions unlike anything else. In addition to being a meditative practice, for me, dancing is also an enormously healing tool for moving through self-consciousness and self-worthiness. Every chance I get to move in a way that feels good for me, in spite of how I may look and in spite of what I think anyone else may think of me for doing it, aligns me with my highest good and helps me embody incredibly potent self-love.

GETTING COMMITTED TO A PRACTICE

So, with infinite ways to meditate, how can you start from where you are? Figure out what works for you, and cultivate a practice that's all your own. Find a community to meditate with. Invite your friends. Join a class. Try a new app that can expand your awareness around new practices. Read about different philosophies and techniques. Trust your intuition to guide you to precisely what you'll be most supported by in the most graceful, easeful way. In other words, just do it. And commit to doing a daily practice, especially if you're just getting started. It may feel uncomfortable at first but trust me, it's one of the best things you can do for your energetic body, your soul, your spirit—really, all dimensions of your being will benefit from a consistent practice.

CLEAR TOXICITY ON ALL LEVELS

Now that you're more aware of your sensitivity to energy, it's time to get serious about detoxifying stagnant and negative energy from all areas of your life. In fact, welcome to your new number-one priority. Freedom is the name of the game, my love—energetic sovereignty, independence, confidence, and clarity that come with being completely grounded in your own being, free of negativity and stagnation that blocks you from shining at your fullest capacity.

EXERCISE: INSIGHT MEDITATION TECHNIQUE

This practice encompasses a comprehensive tool set for strengthening your multisensory discernment while learning to clearly navigate the emotional, mental, and energetic experiences within you that are happening simultaneously. Perhaps you've heard of Vipassana meditation. Or maybe you've had friends or family participate in long, silent meditation retreats (those are typically of the Vipassana variety). Vipassana simply refers to the practice of paying close attention to your sensations rising and falling to see through to your true nature—being a witness to your true self. Vipassana comes from the Buddhist tradition and is even thought to be what the Buddha himself practiced while meditating underneath his famed bodhi tree.

I am going to be sharing with you my take on this ancient practice, which is based on my own experiences inspired by retreats, my personal study, and in guiding individuals and groups (specifically with the Deep Mindfulness Collective in New York City and Shinzen Young, author of *The Science of Enlightenment*).

1. This practice can be done either while sitting or walking (or moving mindfully in any way that feels right for you), but if it's your first time trying this, I recommend following the sitting practice first to familiarize yourself with the flow.

2. Find a comfortable place to sit for at least twenty minutes. This can be on a meditation cushion with your legs crossed, on the couch, or sitting upright in another comfortable position that feels supported. Make sure you are sitting upright with your spine elongated and straight, as this practice is best done while you're highly alert as opposed to lying down.

3. If you're able to do this practice in nature, that is ideal—and you can truly tune into the ancient practice as suggested by the

Buddha himself, who always prescribed meditating under a tree or going into the forest to absorb the calming, soothing energy.

4. Once you're in position, do your best to stay as still as possible so you can really dedicate your focused energy to starting to discern your sensory experience. Make sure you're comfortable enough to not move for twenty minutes or more as you fully commit to this practice.

5. Breathe normally, at first paying attention to the rise and fall of your abdomen as you breathe in and out.

6. You will start to become aware of your senses. Perhaps your mind will start firing off some ideas or narratives; perhaps you'll feel a sensation in a certain part of your body. Feel it all, but as you feel it, remember this practice is to *acknowledge* the feeling as opposed to *engage* with it. You may find that at first in starting this practice you notice a ton of sensations happening at once, but a gift of this practice is that with continued commitment you will start to see how you truly are experiencing one thing at a time. You'll also learn to slow down your receptivity of the information depending on your level of concentration. In other words, you can create a state of calm and therefore clearer discernment within your multiple senses.

7. To acknowledge whatever it is that's coming up for you, you can employ a variety of labels to help you discern what kinds of sensations are present for you as they flow in one by one. So, what's labeling? This is your key tool of insight practice for starting to acknowledge what kinds of senses you have coming up. (Note: the following meditation is inspired by my practice with Shinzen Young and the Deep Mindfulness Collective in New York City. Shinzen's book *The Science of Enlightenment,* as well as long retreats with Janusz Welin and Rakhel Shapiro, were incredibly

enlightening supports for my personal meditation practice, particularly when it comes to the particular style I outline here.)

- When you hear something outside of your being—such as a noise outside or something moving in the room you're in—you can silently label it "hear out."
- When you hear something internally such as an internal dialogue of the mind or another kind of idea or thought popping up in your cognitive space, you can silently label this sensation "hear in."
- When you feel something in your body, this is labeled "feel in," whereas any feeling outside of you such as wind on your skin or an itch on top of your clothing is labeled "feel out."
- If you see visions or pictures appearing in your conscious awareness even with your eyes closed—perhaps you have the sense of a visual image being produced by your clairvoyant abilities—you label this experience as "see in."
- You likely won't see anything outside of you meriting the "see out" label since your eyes are closed, but if you are doing this practice while walking or mindfully moving you can then use this label to discern when you are focusing your conscious awareness on something outside of you.

8. If your attention wanders, which is more than likely, you can simply bring your attention back to your breath and label the rising and falling motion of your abdomen as "rising" and "falling" before you start your labeling practice once more. You can also label "thinking" if you notice your mind trailing off into a particularly intricate narrative you'd like to disassociate from to return to your practice.
9. If you can commit for the full twenty minutes of labeling your senses as you are aware of them, you will notice immediate

effects of deepened relaxation, amplified sensory perception, a heightened sense of intuition, and a laser-focused capacity of concentration. With amplified senses, try enjoying a nourishing activity that feels amazing to your body and soul after this kind of meditation: have your favorite snack, dance, hug someone you love, listen to music—see how you feel!

10. This is a powerful practice that builds on itself over time and can be deepened in many other directions. You can try it out while moving, mindfully walking, or doing another kind of gentle motion that feels supportive to you in diving deeper in concentration and connection to your being. You can also practice this intermittently throughout your day by choosing to tune into the practice for a few minutes here and there to bring yourself back to center when you would like to bring about an immediate grounding sensation.

To learn more about this practice, I highly recommend looking into local meditation community gatherings and classes in your area, meditation retreats, and online guided meditation experiences and teachings that can support your path. You can always tune into the resources I've mentioned in this chapter as well as in the Resources section.

WHAT IS A LIFE DETOX?

What does detoxing your life entail, exactly? It might sound like a huge undertaking, but trust me, it's one of the most worthwhile things you'll do for yourself as an empath.

In order to become a master of your own energy (and fully utilize your intuition and gifts with excellent ease, like you deserve to), an initial deep-dive cleansing period is required. And no, I don't mean a juice cleanse. Your life cleanse will allow you to truly become familiarized with yourself at a deeper level than you've ever imagined. Think of this invitation as your own internal retreat, in which you render yourself free from outside influences and energy drains.

It's time to immediately detoxify your life of anything, anyone, and any environment that doesn't leave you feeling supported to live your very best life. Remember, you deserve the best. And now that you have a better idea of your internal makeup and what you're really working with, you're responsible for giving yourself a solid foundation upon which to truly thrive. You'll soon see how so much refreshed energy is awaiting you right on the other side of letting go of everything that's not really supporting you to live your best life possible. From now on, you get to choose.

DILLON'S EMPATH EXPERIENCE

For much of my life, I used to wake up and just feel the weight of the world on my shoulders. I felt depressed and depleted for no apparent reason most of the time. But I would find reasons to explain how I felt almost as though I needed to collect material evidence to explain why I was feeling so low. What I was experiencing, unbeknownst to me, was a profound heaviness and pain emanating from the collective consciousness.

Before I started meditating and practicing yoga more consistently, I was essentially walking around the world like a sponge, taking in absolutely anything and everything in my path. Being a sponge for the entire collective consciousness is exhausting to say the least. I was guided to practice more yoga and meditation by many people in my life over the years, but I really committed upon the recommendation of my therapist, who was a huge advocate for mindfulness practice.

In yoga and meditation, I learned about my energy body and on top of that, how to protect my energy and actually understand what it felt like to be in my own energy as opposed to being open to absorb energy from everything and everyone around me. I learned about energetic boundaries and protecting my aura, which I'm so grateful is now a default practice of mine that I do almost without having to think about it.

Everything started with a simple willingness to learn some new tools and take suggestions from teachers and guides who I knew could help me cultivate a deeper sense of freedom and independence. It's amazing to me how natural meditation has become, especially when I remember back to when I first started and how difficult it was to sit still with myself. After continuing to practice and receiving support in deepening my practice, I now understand that my entire being is essentially wired to meditate and exist within optimal energetic flow.

WHAT NEEDS TO BE DETOXED?

If you've been living as an unidentified empath for quite a while, chances are you've attracted a large range of relationships, situations, obligations, and repetitive patterns that aren't fully serving you. That's what you need to detox from.

As I shared earlier, because I was so energetically sensitive from such a young age, I developed many survival skills early on in life to cope and provide myself with what I thought I needed at the time. A huge survival skill I learned was a very codependent type of attachment in relationships that helped me feel fulfilled and useful so long as I knew I was helping others, often before giving my own well-being any thought whatsoever. The resulting behavior patterns left me in a cycle of exhaustion and immense energetic drain for quite a while. But I didn't know any other way.

Everything changed when I received my first assignment to intentionally spend time with myself—unstructured time especially so I could finally let my intuition guide me to explore precisely what my soul was really craving to experience. As I did this, I became more sensitive to how much I had been overscheduling time with people or going to places that I didn't really want to go. It turned out I had actually been letting other people make decisions for me, by giving my power of choice over to them.

As I prioritized my own energy more and more, I became acutely aware of friends and even acquaintances who really didn't seem to value me, who instead loved to spend time with me mainly to share their issues and challenges because they knew I would help them feel better. In fact, I had become a magnet for people carrying a lot of darkness and pain who would seek out my presence in order to unload their woes. I was like a sponge, soaking up the emotional baggage of others so they didn't need to bear the weight alone. I subconsciously wanted others to feel better, so I'd simply take away whatever was weighing them down. But in all those years in which I had been trying to take care of everyone else, I had neglected myself completely. I was carrying around stagnant energy, other people's emotional baggage, and internal confusion that was literally weighing me down—more than I was even aware of. Plus, this heaviness and recurring tendency to neglect myself to instead care for others fueled my desire to drink and use drugs in order to check out of my life. When it came to detoxing my life of all the toxicity I had accumulated over the years on multiple levels, I was a prime candidate for a major overhaul.

DETOXING, STEP BY STEP

So now let's get to work! Here's a step-by-step process to detox your life of all that no longer serves you in living your absolute best life:

1. Dedicate about an hour or so to journaling all the people, places, things, commitments, and environments you find yourself involved in that don't feel like they absolutely support you and nourish you in all the ways you really desire.

2. Let your stream of consciousness flow and guide you to identify precisely what it is you are ready to detox from your life. If you need a jump-start, ask yourself these questions:

   • Who leaves me feeling tired after our interactions?
   • Are there places I find myself going to that leave me feeling exhausted afterward?
   • Are there commitments I am showing up for that make me feel drained or depleted in any way?

3. Once you have your list of people, places, things, commitments, activities, and so on, it's time to start taking intentional action to cleanse these elements from your energy. What can you let go of immediately? Is it a relationship that's constantly imbalanced? An environment that's emotionally draining for you? A commitment that takes more from you than you get from it?

I'll give you some support on the key areas to investigate as well as some insight into how you can let go of what really isn't serving your highest good.

EXERCISE: ENERGY HEALING MEDITATION

Did you know that you have everything you need within you already to heal and soothe yourself in the ways your body most desires? You really do; you are that powerful. You are your own best healer and you have the best medicine for you that only you know how to give to yourself in the most perfect way. Your body always strives to be in balance; that's what it's built for. You can expedite the process by following this beautiful healing, self-loving practice as often as you can to clear your body of stagnant energy, toxicity, negativity, and anything that doesn't support your absolute highest good.

1. You can totally enjoy this practice lying down or sitting up if you prefer, but I personally love doing this practice as I am falling asleep—what a beautiful gift to give yourself before going to bed. Plus, talk about powerful subconscious rewiring going on with such a potent infusion of self-love and healing!

2. This practice can last as long as you want, but I encourage you to commit to trying it consistently for at least ten minutes while you're first getting accustomed to what feels good for you. (You'll likely want to do this for longer, possibly even a whole hour!)

3. You can put on meditative music—Reiki playlists on *Spotify* and *YouTube* are great to tune into, or perhaps a healing mantra playlist that includes soothing yoga or kundalini chanting music. Binaural beats and other sound healing tracks set to specific prescriptive frequencies might also resonate with you. Silence is also fine. Use whatever helps you to deeply relax and feel centered, especially before bed if that's when you are doing this practice.

4. Breathe in as deeply as you possibly can, deeper than you have all day long—as though you are breathing in from the heels of your feet to the crown of your head. Hold your breath slightly at

the top of your inhale for a few counts and then fully release with an audible exhale, letting everything go. Do that for at least five rounds of breathing or until you feel deeply centered and calm in your being.

5. As you are breathing, start to tune into your intentions for healing. What parts of your body require healing and peace? What other intentions would you like to infuse into your system? You can create anything you want, anything that is in service to your highest good and optimal well-being.

6. Start by rubbing your palms together rather vigorously until you feel heat generated between them for at least a few seconds. You should feel a strong energetic current you've just created between both palms when you finally stop moving them and briefly move them apart from each other. Can you feel the energy current?

7. Now you can begin the energy healing. Start by placing your palms across your face, covering both of your eyes. Feel the energy streaming from your palms, which are an extension of your heart (they are connected along the same energetic meridian), envisioning your healing, loving energy emanating through your palms and moving throughout the rest of your body.

8. Intuitively move your palms to other spaces on your body that require healing. You know where to go. You can also follow traditional Reiki hand placement recommendations, which go from the top of your head to the bottom of your feet—you can investigate the positioning if you're called to do a more intensive session, or simply follow your intuition and allow your palms and heart to guide you in giving yourself precisely what you need. Your body knows. Just allow yourself to listen.

9. As you are sending yourself healing energy, you can envision your palms channeling healing, white light, a love-filled energy from your

own heart and from source energy (or whatever higher guidance you believe in—this is YOUR practice, so cultivate whatever understanding feels most supportive) throughout your entire being. If you are healing a specific injury, hold the vision of your cells healing rapidly and vibrating in optimal harmony and well-being.

10. By now you've likely fallen asleep or you're deeply relaxed and ready to meditate some more or move into another gentle self-care practice. Do what feels best for you.

11. You can even try this with friends, family, or other individuals you have conscious consent to share this practice with. See how it goes and always share with the intention of spreading love and healing—with this as your focus, you'll never go wrong.

Like everything else in this book, make this your own. It's *your* life after all; it's *your* practice. It's your ceremony made up of your beautiful rituals. And the point of it all is to enjoy it as much as you can. We're here to have fun! There's no right way to do any of this except to be honest with yourself about actually trying the practices that really resonate with you. Are you all in with allowing yourself to be open to new experiences that will surely catalyze your continued expansion, awakening, and healing? You deserve it.

For more information on energy healing, feel free to research your local holistic healing center or anywhere else close to you that offers therapeutic massage, acupuncture, Reiki, other forms of energetic bodywork, and yoga. Have fun playing with your superpowers!

PROTECT YOURSELF (BEFORE YOU WRECK YOURSELF)

As an empath you're probably not a stranger to feeling like you've had your energy completely drained. Maybe it's happened after:

- Hanging out with a needy friend or family member who couldn't stop telling you about his latest stress-inducing drama seemingly without end, depending on your unwavering positivity and loving presence to make him feel better.
- Spending a night out in a crowded restaurant or bar in which the energy just felt particularly chaotic or uneasy.
- Seeing something horrific depicted on the news, especially involving an intensive recapitulation of violence or an unforetold incident of global suffering.
- Witnessing a difficult situation in person, like seeing a homeless person on the street struggling to simply attain a few dollars for his next meal.
- Learning in depth about the real-time statistics of animal endangerment and environmental destruction.

I remember I suffered a particularly bad bout of exhaustion coupled with intense depression in high school after first seeing the film *Amistad*. This film depicts the horrors of slavery, including the separation of families that was commonplace throughout the slave trade. I was so disturbed at viewing this vivid depiction of the worst horrors of humanity that I undertook a renewed sense of responsibility to find some way to correct the wrongs of humanity's past. I wasn't sure how I would do it, but after watching the film unfold, I *had* to do something.

That's what I'm talking about when it comes to protecting your energy. If you've been living your entire life as though you're a sponge for everyone else's emotions—all the good, the bad, the dark, the intense, the heavy, all of it—then it's time to get conscious about protecting your open heart from carrying any additional unintentional burdens. It's not your job to take care of anyone else. Can you imagine that? Especially when you're doing it without any conscious agreement, as you might be doing right now. You get to be free. And you're the one with the keys out of the cage. That's what it feels like, really. When you're an energetic sponge whose entire livelihood has been directed by basing your self-worth and value on of how you make others feel and your ability to help them feel better, it really does feel like being in a cage. Except you don't know you've been in there until you have the awareness that there's another way to live.

So, let's start now. Regardless of where you are on the spectrum of your empath experience, you can learn something about taking care of your energy.

GET SELECTIVE ABOUT YOUR RELATIONSHIPS

Are there any friends, colleagues, family members, or anyone else who comes to mind immediately who are completely draining to be around? Trust your intuition and know that whatever comes up for you is precisely where you're meant to look. Letting go of toxic or draining relationships can feel scary at first, especially if owning your worth and really standing in your value with strong energetic boundaries is new to you. Better late than never, though—it's time to practice really mastering your energy by putting strong boundaries into place, prioritizing your well-being (what feels best for YOU) and incredibly valuable time over all else.

PLATONIC RELATIONSHIPS

One of the first things I did when it came to detoxing my life of all draining relationships was actually less of an intentional action than you might think. Once I became aware of certain people in my life who were draining me through making the list and bringing awareness to them

EXERCISE: CUT ENERGETIC CORDS OF ATTACHMENT

In this exercise you're invited to cut all cords once and for all with anything (and anyone) you've given your power and energy away to. Now is the time to set yourself free from anything that's limiting your ability to move forward. Cut all the cords, clear the slate, release the cellular memory of anything holding you back.

Allow yourself to sink deeply into a meditative state—perhaps following the instructions in the Aura-Shielding Meditation Technique exercise featured at the end of this chapter. While in your meditative state, ask yourself: what cords present in my energy field need to be released? Is something coming up clearly in this moment that needs to be acknowledged immediately? What needs to be let go of in order for you to feel free? Tune in and listen for what comes. Then take a few moments to journal:

- In what ways have you given your power and energy away?
- To whom? To what? And how? To beliefs, to others' expectations (or your own), societal conditioning, fear?
- What are the cords of energy draining you, latching onto you, holding you back from moving forward on your desired path?

Pick at least one person or an idea, an expectation, a belief, or anything you feel is maintaining a powerful energetic pull on you that's holding you back.

Write a letter to your selected entity. In the letter, explain how you are ready to release this entity from your field now and forever. You can trust your intuition to guide whatever else you need to write and what needs to be said to bring closure to this connection. Do you need to express a repressed emotion? Tell this entity something you've always wanted to say? Apologize? Make your negative experience known, if there is one. Say what you wish would have happened instead. Let it all out.

Once you have the letter completed, knowing it contains everything you need to communicate once and for all, read it out loud. Then, depending on how you feel about the situation and how you see closure happening most seamlessly, decide how to destroy it in a demonstration of complete release. You can burn it, beat it up (this is healing for somatic release at the cellular level if you feel like you are angry, upset, or have unexpressed tension to let out), fly it away on a kite... anything your heart truly desires. It's up to you. Trust that your powerful intentions will create the space you truly need.

Be a conscious observer of any resistance that comes up along the way. A lot can come up in this process. This is an incredibly powerful tool that you will probably draw upon again going forward. Take it easy with yourself in this practice as it can bring up a lot of intensity and unfelt emotions that are ready to be felt and released.

Regardless, keep choosing to stand in your full light, power, and freedom. Know that you are infinitely expansive and capable of manifesting anything you truly desire once you are able to shine your brightest light. I see you.

specifically, I was able to make conscious decisions *not* to do things. For example, I stopped making plans with people I identified as exhausting or draining. As a result, a lot of these people naturally fell away from my life as I became less available for soaking up their negativity. Awareness is a powerful tool. Simply by understanding more clearly the relationships I was allowing myself into that felt exhausting, I energetically became less noticeable to the energy vampires that used to find me seemingly out of nowhere. I simply fell out of resonance with them.

Early on in my sobriety—when my emotional experience was incredibly amplified as my emotions and my ability to discern my own energy from that of others started to come into my awareness for the first time—I found it was incredibly important for me to spend time only with a rather small group of people I knew could support me. Despite feeling comfortable for most of my life in big groups, at loud, busy parties and in rather chaotic situations, as I was coming back to myself and learning about my own energy, I found hanging out even with just one friend and being able to go deep into our connection together the most nourishing experience I could have hoped for. I surprise myself even to this day sometimes with how much I enjoy spending time alone and also with smaller, more intimate groups.

ROMANTIC RELATIONSHIPS

I also found it very helpful to commit to not dating for about a year while I really got to know myself for what felt like the first time. "Dating myself" was a detoxifying experience because there were many occasions on which I might have opted to spend time with a date or intimate partner, but instead I chose to spend time with myself, taking myself on dates, and really getting to know what I enjoyed most about life. What was it that lit me up? What did I want to do when I really tuned in and asked myself precisely that? Listening to my deepest desires in this intuitive way was such a powerful skill that is now the foundation of everything else I do. As long as I am putting myself and my happiness and feeling of positive well-being first, everything else falls into place.

Want to know what's even more magical? I was initially terrified of dating myself for a year because I had been so accustomed to being in long-term relationships! But once I really started focusing my attention on myself, which even at times meant turning down invitations and date propositions when those really didn't feel aligned with my highest good, I actually started attracting a whole new array of people into my life. Talk about upgrades—suddenly a whole new kind of dating scene emerged that I had never been aware of prior. Once I started becoming more powerful in my own energetic discernment and showed up in life with clearer boundaries, I attracted people who mirrored that same experience back to me. I started becoming available for entirely new kinds of relationships with people who had healthy boundaries, good self-esteem, and self-worth.

CHOOSE YOUR COMMITMENTS WISELY

A particularly great way to practice self-care is to treat yourself like the most important person in your life, because guess what? You are. As such, your time needs to be treated with the utmost value and care. How are you spending your time? Are you doing things that leave you feeling exhausted, like you're just doing them because other people expect certain things of you? Now you get to choose how you spend your time. You get to stop doing anything you don't really want to do. Anything that doesn't empower you, nourish you, or support you deeply needs to go.

Does that sound dramatic to you? It might be, and I understand that many of you reading these words may be parents, caregivers, involved in taxing careers—the list goes on and on ad infinitum. You are busy, that's for sure—but I'm here to remind you that you always have a choice, no matter what, regarding how you allow yourself to feel and whether your life is set up to support you in how you truly desire to feel. You are such a powerful creator, and I won't hold you to anything less even if it's hard to see yourself that way because for so long you've been so used to taking care of everyone else before yourself. I'm here to remind you that the best thing you can do not only for yourself but for everyone else is to start putting you first in every way—that's how you strengthen your capacity to serve in alignment with your soul calling. That's the key to living a fulfilling, impactful, loving life. I promise.

So tell me, are there a lot of things in your life at this moment that you're invested in that feel exhausting? Don't fret, just take a moment and reflect: why are you showing up to be invested in obligations and commitments that don't really serve you? What's your actual motive? Do you feel like you have to? Like you have no choice? Are you feeling triggered by the invitation I am offering you to take an honest look at your life and really discern any ways in which you're allowing yourself to be drained? What's underneath the trigger—what is the actual lesson to be learned? What would it be like to stop making excuses and instead declare what you truly desire and simply give that to yourself, knowing you have the capacity to do so? You've had it all along.

You'll quickly find that by pausing and asking yourself these simple questions you'll start to identify the underlying reasons you're involved in particular circumstances. With your new awareness, you have so much power to make a choice that's in complete integrity.

Nothing is more empowering or supportive than living life truly aligned with what you value and believe. This is the precise definition of alignment, which is simply another word for integrity. You're on a path to learning how integrity is a top priority in your life, alongside treating yourself like the most important person in your life. As long as you consistently strive to attend to these two elements as often as you possibly can, you'll find that your life is able to shift in incredible, often enormously positive, ways.

REASSESSING YOUR COMMITMENTS

If you've been used to saying yes to everyone else for your entire life, it's time to get used to saying no more often. Say no to things that:

- Don't totally align with your spirit
- Don't feed your soul
- You might simply be doing to please others
- Make you feel out of integrity with your true desires

How do you get yourself out of commitments? Stop doing things you don't want to do. Simple as that. Say no to invitations and commitments if you don't really want to be somewhere or do something. Don't waste time worrying about what other people are going to think about you. Remember: you're here to put yourself first.

When it comes to saying no, there are so many ways to communicate your desires clearly without being hurtful or too abrupt, which was precisely what I used to be afraid of when I first learned that I actually had permission to say no to things I didn't genuinely want to do. I used to be so afraid of hurting other people's feelings, letting them down, or saying no in a way that felt really rude. What I learned is that more often than not people, especially those who care most about you, appreciate your honesty more than anything. The more clearly you can communicate what you truly desire in a thoughtful way the better. If you are invited to attend an event that your heart isn't really invested in—a great way to clearly communicate this truth to your friend is to say something along the lines of: "Thank you so much for the invitation. I appreciate your consideration and for thinking of me, and you know I love spending time with you! But my heart isn't feeling genuinely invested in this event, so I'm going to pass for now. Please keep me in mind for future gatherings though." Your true friends will get it—and they'll appreciate you being honest, knowing that when you commit to future invitations you're fully present and truly desire being there. Your friends desire your full presence—not a half-assed attempt at showing up in which your energy clearly wants to be somewhere else. Communicating your desires clearly in this way is a beautiful practice in embodying the utmost integrity.

If you notice that putting yourself first is incredibly challenging, pause in the moments you feel uncomfortable and be there to support yourself, asking yourself why you feel uncomfortable, what's being activated for you, and what might there be to learn from this feeling. Underneath the discomfort, especially if you find that it's stemming from a fear of making someone else uncomfortable or letting others down, is a beautiful space for you to expand into, in full integrity and power. How can you give yourself what you need? How can you powerfully express your truth despite how it might affect others? This is your life, after all. How are you choosing to spend your time and energy?

You'll see that the more you practice pausing when you feel discomfort, the easier it gets to trust that whatever it is that feels hard will soon pass. Your years of programming yourself to do things to make other people feel good or to meet other people's expectations likely runs deep if this challenge feels triggering for you. Give yourself time to acclimate and practice by not scheduling things too far in advance.

Intentionally leave open space on your calendar to see what flows more naturally to fill your time. Trust that new opportunities perfectly meant for you will come at precisely the right times. The more I listened to what I really wanted in the moment, the more I found that I was receiving invitations to events, parties, and intimate gatherings that really suited my needs. It became less and less common for me to end up in places that didn't really agree with me and likewise I found myself having to turn down fewer invitations for things I didn't want to do. When your life feels easeful and in flow, you know you are honoring yourself and truly putting yourself first. When you start to clear space in your life for the commitments that most matter to you, you'll notice that more aligned opportunities will more regularly present themselves to you. Like attracts like, just like that. And the letting go and saying no gets easier over time. Trust that practice in this case definitely makes perfect; perfection, in this case, is being you, living your beautifully designed, aligned, and flowing life.

DROPPING COMMITMENTS IS EASIER THAN YOU THINK

I learned early on in my life to show up for others, before ever considering if I actually wanted to do something. I had no regard for myself, but it was unconscious because I had no awareness or insight into why considering my own needs first was important. The way this phenomenon took shape most often was again rooted in relationships, but it was also connected to the events I was overcommitting to because of what I thought others expected of me. Even if I didn't want to do something, I went, because I was too concerned with looking good. I never wanted to be associated with being a flake. My image and what I understood people to see me as was my number one currency in life—it meant that I was valuable so long as I kept it intact. This was all prior to having developed any of my own internally sourced self-esteem and self-worth. Of course I had to show up for the party I committed to going to months ago, even when the date came and I didn't feel like going at all. What would people think if I were to cancel?

I remember this type of scenario used to feel absolutely unbearable to me. How could I let other people down? Well, there were many layers at play here that I started to dismantle in order to create an easier, more peaceful sense of flow with space to move in my life. A huge lesson in my empath journey has been learning to trust that leaving time open for spontaneity is key to allowing myself to experience just how supportive the universe really is of my every move.

Once I started getting more in touch with my emotions as well as intentionally managing my own energy, I naturally found myself needing to cancel commitments and what I thought were obligations I had signed on to months prior that no longer felt relevant to me. I was terrified of what other people would think of me for backing out of dinners, events, retreats, and other social commitments. What I found was a complete surprise. I walked directly into the terrifying tasks at hand expecting to be faced with total rejection, but instead I was met mostly with understanding and even more so with relief.

Unless you are capable of saying no, your yes is meaningless.
—Osho

I loved seeing how many times after I changed my mind about something I had committed to, how relieved the other parties were to find that I felt the same way they did. You see, when I was tuned into feeling that something was no longer a good fit for me, chances were fairly good that the other people I was going to commune with were feeling similarly and wanted to cancel as well or wanted permission to change the date. They were feeling the same way I was with respect to maintaining an appearance of integrity without really saying how they actually felt. We are all trying to impress each other, even at times at the expense of not expressing our full truth.

What I've found extremely empowering along my empath journey is that I get to be the one who gives so much permission to others to simply feel how they really feel and stand in their truth, usually by paving the way to say what I'm really feeling first. I love being the mirror for others' experience that allows them to be who they really are, because finally someone else feels what they are really feeling. What if we all honored our highest truth and only answered our yeses and nos in full integrity? I'm excited envisioning what kind of world we can cocreate together when that's the natural state of being.

SAYING NO ALLOWS YOUR YESES TO BECOME MORE MEANINGFUL

The beautiful thing about saying no more often is that you create space for your more meaningful yeses. Instead of saying yes to everything to please everyone else, you follow only your highest excitement and best feelings so that when you say yes to doing something, you really mean it and are looking forward to it. You are choosing to be fully present, and this type of mindfulness is a powerful mechanism for cultivating deeper self-trust, self-love, and clear energetic boundaries. If you do this for a while in full integrity, you'll find that you'll stop getting invited to things that aren't in your highest alignment, and with the space that's created from your nos you'll become more open to receiving beautiful invitations and opportunities that are even more clear yeses for you.

YOUR ENVIRONMENT IS EVERYTHING

Being a supersensitive energetic being who feels everything going on around you requires a careful sensitivity to the environments you select to engage in. Knowing you can absorb negativity like nobody's business means you have to make sure the environments you enter into are supporting you completely. Are you finding yourself regularly spending time in particular environments that really don't serve you? That make you feel tired? That leave you feeling off? These are some questions to contemplate as you take your initial inventory of what areas of your life qualify for a deep clean.

As an empath, you're likely also sensitive to noise and crowds. As such, you may find that after a bit of practice with actually tuning into your intuition and listening in consciously to hear what you really desire, you prefer to spend time in more peaceful scenarios with less noise and less people in general. You might be surprised to find that even though you've lived in a city for what feels like forever, once you really start prioritizing your well-being, you listen to a deeper pull to go spend more time in nature.

THE POWER OF WATER

Spending as much time as you can immersed in nature, particularly around the ocean, can feel immensely healing. I've found in my experience an incredibly powerful healing happens whenever I surround myself in mountainous, forest-covered areas. Something about being completely embedded in trees and expansive natural life is not only incredibly grounding for my being, but feels like it also has the effect of cleansing my energy by soaking in anything that's not mine.

Diving into the ocean and bathing in the purifying salt water has a similarly powerful effect. Go to nature as much as you can and see how you react. If it fills your soul and makes you feel deeply cleansed and healed, welcome to empath travel life. You'll surely find yourself venturing to similar spaces—in the next town or across the world—in search of new energy centers that fill you in beautiful ways and connect you more deeply to unknown facets of your being.

HOW YOUR ENVIRONMENT AFFECTS YOUR RELATIONSHIPS WITH YOURSELF AND OTHERS

When I started consciously becoming aware of how much my environment affected my energy and overall sense of well-being, I found out quite a few things about myself that really surprised me. At first, despite being a party person my entire life who thought she loved nothing more than a crowded, lively house party, I realized I much preferred quiet dinners with a small group of friends or even just one friend compared to any wild nights out. Crowds exhausted me, especially when alcohol was involved. Even if people around me weren't getting wasted, I noticed that just being in an environment in which people were drinking put me off a bit because I so deeply wanted to connect with them intimately and presently, but I found that when others were drinking that wasn't entirely possible. (Years later, after getting more comfortable in my own sobriety, being in situations with alcohol aren't uncomfortable at all. I barely notice because I am so clear on my own energetic boundaries.) I also found that my friends, who had known me as a party person, were actually really relieved at times to find that I preferred to enjoy an intimate dinner or opportunity to connect with them while doing something more low-key.

Changing my environment also had the wonderful side benefit of deepening many of my friendships. It actually felt like some of my friends were waiting for the invitation to deepen our friendship, which happens naturally when you spend actual time together talking and listening and sharing instead of trying to do any of the above amidst loud music and chaotic, distracting social situations.

YOUR ENVIRONMENT AT WORK

Since you probably spend a lot of your time at your workplace or wherever it is you spend time to make your livelihood, it's important to consider these environments as well. Perhaps you have a boss, a team, people you manage, other colleagues you're interacting with on a consistent basis, and other people you coordinate with for various needs. And your environment overall might bring with it particular challenges—for example, being inside all day, especially if there's lackluster lighting and a lack of fresh air, it can be taxing on your body, mind, and spirit for sure. Plus, work requires a lot of navigation when it comes to having healthy relationships and strong energetic boundaries. And when we throw any underlying challenges you may face regarding worthiness and self-esteem into the mix—oh man, work can be especially triggering. I know this was the case for me for many years. So naturally, my professional life was and continues to be a perfect playing ground for exercising self-care, cultivating healthy boundaries, and detoxing energy drains.

I worked in advertising and public relations in varying capacities for many years prior to taking the leap into entrepreneurship to start my own company. The more sensitive I became to my preferences and the more my empathic gifts developed, eventually the desire within me to leave my job became too loud to ignore. Even though I had been working in an office for years and had become comfortable thinking that perhaps I'd always be in one, eventually I admitted that I didn't actually like sitting inside all day at a desk surrounded by so many different personalities that I was subconsciously mitigating all day long.

In my last full-time job, the other experience that catalyzed my departure was the feeling of needing to intentionally dim my light in order to accommodate others' apparent suppression of their own light. The more sensitive I became to my empathic gifts and intuitive abilities, while also making a concerted effort to pursue various forms of healing, transformational development, and training in my own right, the more difficult I found it to abide by the rules that office culture outlined. Not only that, but I experienced an entirely different view of my empathic tendency to care for others before myself because of the subtleties of office communication and behavior protocol.

For example, even though I would have the most incredible experiences outside of the office, in conversation with coworkers about our weekends I would often find myself censoring or diluting my full explanation of what I had experienced because I could already sense that they hadn't had nearly as much fun as I had. I could tell they were feeling some disappointment as they reflected on their experiences.

Who knows if what I was sensing in my coworkers was accurate or not, but regardless, my nearly automatic response to dilute myself in order to accommodate them reminded me of my old behavior, which I hadn't been accustomed to acting on for a very long time. Ultimately I felt overly conscious of appearing to be too extraordinary in a way that might feel isolating to my coworkers. After all, we needed to perform as a unit and I didn't want to do anything to threaten that dynamic so long as I was embedded in the culture.

Looking back, this experience was all perfectly aligned to help me tune into the needed motivation to leave my job and start my own company, which effectively lead me to this moment right now here with you. I followed my intuition and finally listened to what had been guiding me for quite a long time to take the leap into the unknown and really trust that I deserved to expand to my fullest capacity of light and fullest expression of my unique gifts.

GETTING CLEAR ON WHAT'S YOURS: LEARNING DISCERNMENT

Living a fully empowered life with your empathic gifts requires you to get in touch with your feelings as clearly as possible. For empaths, this task can be quite difficult because you need to develop a strong capacity for discernment. In this context, I use discernment to mean sorting out what's energetically yours, and what is energy from elsewhere that you have been carrying as your own for quite some time. The beautiful thing about discernment is that as you continue to refine your practice, you will find that you become less available for absorbing any unwanted energies from outside of yourself.

Discernment may seem like a tall order if you are new to the concept of being able to choose what you interact with energetically instead of letting everything impact you or stick to you like glue. Trust your innate power and let your intuition start guiding you in developing your discernment skills. Your goal is not only to protect yourself energetically, but also to create stronger boundaries so that "energy vampires" are less likely to prey upon you or drain you.

WHAT ARE ENERGY VAMPIRES?

First things first. What is an energy vampire? This term refers to someone who is unconsciously drawn to empaths and other beings who present themselves as very open, giving, caring, and considerate as a target for offloading their energetic waste. This waste can materialize as sadness, anxiety, anger—really anything they desire getting rid of. Energy vampires may present themselves as stressed out, pessimistic downers who lack empathy and may also often blame others from a victimized stance. Like the spectrum of human diversity, the same is true for energy vampires—they come in all shapes, sizes, and ages.

There are only two kinds of people who can drain your energy: those you love, and those you fear. In both instances it is you who let them in. They did not force their way into your aura, or pry their way into your reality experience.

—Anthon St. Maarten

Energy vampires are drawn to empaths in particular because energetically they can sense that empaths can absorb their negativity, while also serving as their prey, so the vampire can proverbially suck the life (positivity, love, caring energy) out of them. If this is all happening subconsciously, which is very often the case, this dynamic can persist for lengthy periods while materializing for the empath involved as constant physical or emotional drain, a distinct feeling of not being treated fairly or being taken advantage of, and intense exhaustion or sadness. The empath involved may feel confused as to why emotions that don't seem to be their own keep coming up, as though they are somehow experiencing someone else's emotional baggage. This is precisely what's happened, and actually describes perfectly what my catalyst was for seeking out support in clearing my energy through my first Reiki session.

If you identify as an empath, chances are you've encountered energy vampires to varying degrees in multiple facets of your life—especially in your romantic relationships, with certain family members, or even coworkers. If you've experienced this type of draining exchange before, I'm here to share with you how you have an incredibly powerful ability to course correct once you know what you're dealing with.

PROTECT YOURSELF FROM ENERGY VAMPIRES

As soon as you create clear boundaries around your energy, you will feel an immediate shift with regard to the types of people you attract into your life. If you're used to attracting people who are needy, depressed, looking to offload their anxiety on you, and blaming things outside of themselves for their current circumstances (while looking at you to cosign their story), it's time to stop the cycle now and forever. You can do so in one simple step: claim your energetic sovereignty now and in this moment commit to protecting yourself from being taken advantage of ever again.

Now that you've made your commitment, let's see how it can manifest. What does it mean to be energetically sovereign? It means that you are impenetrable by any foreign entities or energies outside of you. You are in complete control of your energy and what goes in and out. To fully embody your sovereignty, you are invited to commit completely to radical self-care (using the many techniques outlined in this book is a great way to start), healing your self-worth and self-esteem, and more than anything, doing your daily energetic practice to ensure your energetic boundaries are in alignment with what's best for you. That means you might:

- Meditate daily
- Practice your daily rituals
- Become familiar with aura shielding and protection techniques (more on that in the next exercise)
- Check in with your energy frequently, especially in energetically difficult situations
- Commit to living your most extraordinary life for you and no one else

CONDUCT ENERGY CHECK-INS

A powerful practice for strengthening your discernment abilities while also creating clear energetic boundaries within your own sovereignty is to simply start asking yourself the following as often as possible but especially in social situations:

- How am I feeling right now in this moment?
- How is this situation impacting me?
- How are the people around me interacting with me?
- Do I feel nourished? Do I feel drained?

This is a simple practice that will strengthen your connection to yourself and your own intuitive discernment abilities. You can listen to yourself and give yourself what you need. The more you give yourself what you need, the clearer your energetic boundaries will be drawn and the less susceptible you will be to energy vampires and to feeling drained by situations that aren't aligned with your highest good.

EXERCISE: AURA-SHIELDING MEDITATION TECHNIQUE

Aura-cleansing meditation and visualizations are amazingly healing. And there are infinite ways to do them. The key is to figure out what works best for you and perhaps cultivate your own version that feels most supportive. Here is one of my favorite ways to practice this healing, energizing routine:

1. Find a quiet, peaceful space to sit for a few minutes, perhaps in your sacred meditation space or outside in nature.

2. Set a timer for a few minutes if it's helpful for you to be fully present to the experience. Try ten minutes to start and feel free to go for longer if you so desire.

3. Breathe deeply, deeper than you have all day long—envisioning pulling earth energy up through your heels all the way up through your body to the crown of your head. As you inhale, hold your breath for a few counts at the top until you can't hold it any longer. Then let everything go, allowing any tension to melt away completely. Follow this cycle for five more breaths.

4. As you are breathing, begin envisioning cleansing white light dripping over you in all directions, emanating from the sun above, from source energy, from whatever source of healing energy you believe in and most resonate with.

5. As the light pours over you in all directions, picture the healing light removing anything that no longer serves you as it fills your energy field and helps cleanse it of everything blocking you from connection with your true self.

6. You can picture anything that is not yours being cleared away, simply falling off of you and being removed from within you as it's released to the earth where its recycled energetically as clear, loving light.

7. You can infuse intentions into this healing practice as well by bringing to mind your favorite mantras (affirmative statements you repeat aloud or to yourself) or prayers that feel healing and empowering for you to tune into deeply. Say the mantras and/or prayers as you envision the light covering your aura and protecting you with a strong shield of beautiful loving energy. Envision the mantras written within the light, solidified into your consciousness from now on.

Make this exercise your own. Perhaps you have specific guides you'd like to connect with to assist in your aura strengthening. Perhaps you have an added component of visualization, such as traveling in your imagination to your sacred dream-world space, filled with healing energy. Everyone will have a different style that works for them; the important thing is to stay committed to a practice that inspires you, grounds you, and excites you by supporting a stronger connection to yourself and your unique capacity to feel deeply.

CHAPTER 5
Lifelong Expression and Expansion

After I celebrated five years sober, I moved to Bali, following my soul's calling to explore a place I had always dreamed about visiting. After touching down the first day on the sacred island—appropriately referred to as the Island of the Gods—I immediately knew I would be staying for longer than planned. When I arrived, it genuinely felt like I was being guided to be there at that specific moment in time.

I met my soul family on the dance floor, at any one of my favorite cafés, at the market, at a sound bath—we are like magnets for one another. We were meant to find each other; we were meant to help each other grow and activate one another into new levels of transformation and healing. It happened so frequently that I would catch someone's eye—someone I had never seen before until that moment—and we would lock our gaze, as though we were remembering what other lifetimes we had spent together and what we might have been doing in that other story.

I came to expect this type of connection to arise fairly often, and I felt extremely grateful for the familiarity I would feel with new friends instantaneously, knowing we were being guided toward supporting one another's journey going forward. I found it helpful to acknowledge how with many of these new connections I wasn't ready to meet them until the moment in which we connected. In many cases if we had even come across each other a month or two before, we wouldn't have been in resonance. We were magnetized to each other in divine time because we were in resonance and therefore able to really connect and share our gifts.

CELEBRATE THE MIRACLES IN EVERY MOMENT

Welcome home. You're in this adventure for the long haul, my friend, ripe with continued expansion, deeper expression of your gifts, and embodiment of your fullest, most unique power. You're destined for absolute greatness, nothing less. Can you feel it? Your whole life awaits—the grandest adventure of all time indeed. Thank you for choosing to be here on such a beautiful, divinely guided path. Thank you for choosing to show up in only the ways that you can to share the gifts your soul is designed to bring forth. You really could have been anywhere else right now, but instead you're here reading these words, choosing to perhaps take on a new perspective in life. You are so powerful, so courageous, and so ready. I see you.

As you prepare to embark on an abundance and joy-filled journey into your most nourishing life, consider the following tools and tips forthcoming in the next section that will guide you in anchoring even more deeply into your new perspective. Get ready to receive all the inspiration you need to call in your soul tribe, create incredible community, and most of all, ensure you're fully supported in integrating your next-level transformation and continued expansion.

MAGNETIZE YOUR TRIBE

Connecting to your own community of conscious friends and collaborators who are like-minded and uplifting is a great asset to an empath. Chances are, you're already surrounded by plenty of just these kinds of people—your people! We're magnets for each other. I love this Erykah Badu quote: "I think people who vibrate at the same frequency, vibrate toward each other. They call it, in science, sympathetic vibrations." Amen, sis. She's talking about our energy and how like attracts like.

Our cells seek the same vibration elsewhere, to be in resonance. But if you're just getting into this awareness, maybe you need to make some more proactive steps toward cultivating this loving, supportive, conscious community that can elevate you and be there for you when you need help, have questions, or want to delve deeper into a topic. And sometimes this community arises with cleansing and clearing your life of all toxicity. Making space for new relationships, new activities, and perhaps even a new livelihood to emerge will all be a part of your adventure as an empath. When you start to live with deeper meaning and connection, things will naturally start to change in more ways than you can imagine.

Even if you've felt like no one has really ever understood you, you are not alone. There are so many people on this planet, on this path, on your same awakening journey, going through it just like you. You may think you've had a really hard time, but so many other souls have had the same experience. In fact, your soul family is looking for you. They are all over the world at this moment, doing their transformational work, preparing to one day be in resonance with you.

FINDING YOUR SOUL FAMILY

As an empath it's so important to let go of what no longer serves your highest good, especially while you are on a rapid trajectory of growth and expansion. The more you can let go of what's not in resonance with you, the more space you allow for what is better aligned with you to enter into your life, most often in incredibly synchronistic, supportive ways. Letting go of old relationships or people who were meant to be on your path for a certain time is crucial to allowing yourself to fully magnetize the soul family you are meant to connect with. Your soul connections can't find you if you are hiding out in relationships and communities that aren't actually a reflection of who you really are.

Your soul family sees you. You know it when you first come into contact; you simply feel an instant familiarity. You are destined to cocreate incredible existences together—walking the path of true divine rebels. You are meant to stand out. You aren't meant to follow the crowd. You are here to create the future, which is so much more fun and supportive when you're doing so alongside other visionary creators who see what you see and feel everything along the way too.

Magnetizing your dream tribe, your soul family, is easy when you become clear on what it is you actually want and what you stand for. Let your purpose emanate from all you do and in every way you show up, in constant recommitment to making decisions based on trust and faith while putting yourself first no matter what.

The flip side to growing a dream tribe is that you will naturally let go of some people who were part of your journey pre-awakening. As I grew many people I had been connected to naturally fell away. It was important to let them go as I grew to make space for all the new resonant connections that were meant to come into my path. Letting go of old relationships was at first challenging for me because I had acquired this belief somewhere early on in life that the most desirable thing for me to have was the same group of friends from childhood all the way into adulthood. (I would think of the movie *Now and Then* in which the four girls are best friends from early on and even have a clubhouse that they meet in over the years, even after having their own children.)

Our deepest fear is not that we are inadequate. Our deepest fear is that we are powerful beyond measure. It is our light, not our darkness, that most frightens us. We ask ourselves, Who am I to be brilliant, gorgeous, talented, fabulous? Actually, who are you not to be?
—Marianne Williamson, *A Return to Love*

It can be hard at first to let people go, especially if you're dealing with friends you've known for a long time, and even in some cases family. The most helpful thing I frequently remind myself of in cases where it feels challenging to release relationships that are no longer in alignment with my highest good is that we are all on our own paths and while we may have at one point shared a common destination and resonance, our paths are always evolving and changing—like waves, not straight lines. And like the waves that we are riding as we grow, naturally we simply fall out of resonance with one another here and there, although it's possible for our waves to collide once again in the future, perhaps after substantial transformation has occurred to bring both parties back into resonance. We're not traveling along straight lines that are matched up in parallel forever—we are malleable, flexible, and constantly being molded according to the guidance of our most amplified desires. A huge part of allowing yourself to be fully free to follow your own unique guidance and your most fulfilling path will always include the invitation to let go of the people and connections in general that don't fully support your evolution. You deserve to feel understood. To be met. To be loved.

Letting go doesn't have to be dramatic either. It can be easy and peaceful and polite even. Letting go especially if you're dealing with a friendship can provide an enormously powerful opportunity to exercise your communication skills by declaring what you truly desire, and then aligning your actions to support yourself in achieving your desired state of being. And chances are if you're feeling the call to end a relationship or dial back your involvement with someone or even a community, you speaking your truth is of service to the others involved, as they likely feel the same. Energy is experienced in multiple directions of course—if you feel out of alignment, the people you're connected to feel it as well. Chances are other people involved are just waiting for permission to say the same thing—and how beautiful is it that you can be precisely that permission.

COMMUNITY CAN HELP YOU HEAL AND LEARN

Recovery was the first space in which I really found what I considered to be my tribe. I experienced what it was like to heal and transform alongside other like-minded souls brought together by a common desire to better ourselves and expand our spiritual connection to higher guidance. I joined Alcoholics Anonymous in New York City in the late fall of 2011. Community had always been a part of my life. I had always been intent on bringing people together to share incredible, fun experiences, which was ultimately the underlying motivation of a lot of my partying years. Earlier on in school I had even had stints of activism and community organizing through various clubs and my academic pursuits focused on social movements, revolution, and political economics.

Even through my drinking and drug use, I was always seeking at a deeper level communion not only with the people around me but ultimately with the divine. I didn't know it at the time, or if I did to some extent I wasn't fully conscious of it. For much of my early adolescence and adulthood, until I got sober at age twenty-four, I really couldn't stand being alone. It was the hardest thing for me, because if I was alone, I had to listen to my negative self-talk, which was horrifically abusive and traumatizing.

After a decade or so of seeking community and connection and spirituality in drugs and drinking, I reached such a rock-bottom point of darkness that I had no other choice but to seek support in setting myself free. I didn't know what to do, but I had friends, family, and my therapist at the time referring me to Alcoholics Anonymous, which I had heard of but really had no idea what it'd actually be like. Instead, I had a lot of stereotypical beliefs about what it was—homeless men gathered in a basement talking about how to stay away from their drinking escapades. But I was so desperate, I figured I had nothing to lose if I checked it out; I could always leave.

My experience upon arriving at my first AA meeting was unlike anything I could have expected. I arrived early and saw a ton of cool-looking people my age hanging out on the sidewalk near Union Square, talking and smoking cigarettes. I walked up on the outskirts of the crowd, almost as though I was pretending to pass by. I felt extremely nervous. Here I was and it was all or nothing, time to jump in. A guy immediately caught my eye and asked me if I was there for the AA meeting. I was astonished at him asking me such a question so openly and out loud—I felt embarrassed to be asked such a question out in public. I mustered up the courage to answer him yes, and he immediately connected me with a woman who was standing nearby.

When you change the way you look at things, the things
you look at change.
—Wayne Dyer

The rest of the evening is quite a blur. Even though I was a day or two sober at the time, I was detoxing from so many traumatic experiences and substances that had been occupying my system for years that it was hard for me to be present. I was so overwhelmed and so stuck in my head. But I'll never forget, when I met that woman outside the meeting I immediately felt supported. She guided me to the room where the meeting was happening and invited me to sit right in front of everyone (in the front row facing the meeting). I started crying right away from the overwhelming senses of relief and surrender I felt for finally asking for help, and also in response to the intense feeling of connection and love pervading the room. I had never felt anything like it.

By the end of the meeting I had cried so many tears into my scarf that I ultimately threw it away after the meeting. I was so nervous and raw afterward, like this was it—I had finally given up and I had no idea where I was headed. Thank god someone came over to me and invited me out to the diner to hang out with everyone after the meeting. I pretended at first like I had somewhere else to be, but really I was just so embarrassed that I looked horrible from crying so profusely. I didn't want to be seen at all, let alone in a diner with a bunch of people who just witnessed me falling apart at my first AA meeting.

But something inside of me guided me to say yes and just go. This would be a theme of my experience in recovery—just say yes and go. Let yourself be carried. Trust that spirit is working through these people who are here to help you see yourself, connect to higher guidance, and heal. I went to the diner that night and witnessed how uncomfortable it was for me to even have conversations with people without alcohol, without the loud music of the club bumping in the background, and without dark lights and chaotic energy to distract us. I felt so raw, but again and again people showed me so much kindness and love that I felt instantly healed.

I knew there was something here for me. And sure enough, the woman I was first introduced to outside of the meeting invited me to meet her the next day at another meeting. I thought she was asking me out on a date at the time, but I later realized that she was inviting me to start doing the work of the twelve steps (which are the foundation of the program as outlined in the *Big Book of Alcoholics Anonymous*). And I just kept coming back.

I did the steps a few times, started sponsoring other people in the program, got extremely involved in all facets of the program's service opportunities, and for many years went to multiple meetings a week, even when I traveled outside of the country. I had no idea at the time that I had picked the best place in the world to get sober. With more than four thousand meetings per week, New York City was like a smorgasbord of recovery unlike anywhere else in the world. Before going in I was worried about what I would do for fun when I stopped drinking. I didn't know what there was to do if you didn't spend your weekend in the bars or clubs. I had a lot of learning to do, that was for sure.

I was in awe of how diverse and eclectic recovery was everywhere I went and how in spite of people's external and material differences, we were able to collaborate and cocreate such incredible experiences and deep sustained healing. I witnessed a continuous stream of miracles again and again. It became my new normal. I also loved being able to witness others transform and become completely reborn in front of my own eyes—that was a huge incentive for staying close to the program for so many years. There's nothing like seeing the light come on in someone. Really, it's the most beautiful experience and feeling to witness and celebrate. I witnessed so many rebirths firsthand, which has absolutely been a critical piece of my path leading me to this precise moment. Nothing is more nourishing than seeing others transform in the ways I myself have experienced transformation.

With a seed of willingness to try a new way, take direction, and start to cultivate trust in community, intuition, and all the powers that be outside of your own ego, life beyond your wildest dreams awaits. And the same promise is on offer to all beings, regardless of whether or not you identify with the recovery story. Many recovery stories actually manifest as pain that empaths can identify with—excruciating loneliness, self-abandonment, and an overreliance on letting outside appearance define your own intrinsic sense of self-worth and value.

CALLING IN YOUR SUPPORT TEAM

You have quite a life unfolding right in front of you. You are speaking your most expansive dream realities into being, and feeling your way into embodying your most beautiful, nourishing, soul-filled desires. There is no limit to what you can cocreate as long as you continue your transformation and transmutation of anything that's in the way of aligning to your highest, most authentic truth.

It's sometimes said that you are the average of the five people you spend the most time with. Trust that this is even truer for empaths, and select your tribe wisely. Only align yourself with the best of the best. It's okay to be an energy snob. When you prioritize your well-being above all else, remember that you are being of service to the rest of the planet by contributing to an incredibly powerful resonance and harmonic balance amidst all beings.

You are here to thrive. You are here to inspire others to live their best lives too, simply by witnessing what's possible through your embodied example. You are pure magic, nothing less. And as such, nothing will ensure your continued momentum and transcendence better than genuine, loving support.

What kind of support are we talking about here? Support can take many forms, but some popular choices are life coaching, retreats, workshops, mentors, and the like. We'll talk more about these options in a minute. What else qualifies as support along your path? Your tribe, which we already discussed. Make sure you surround yourself with people who see your vision and see you, who elevate you, and who encourage you to show up fully as yourself. As an empath with clear boundaries who prioritizes your energy and well-being above all else, you'll continue to notice how crucial it is to surround yourself with only the best, most nourishing, loving people you can find. In fact, you'll likely attract them to you the better you take care of yourself— that's how this divine flow works, remember?

INVESTING IN YOURSELF

No matter what type of support you end up choosing for yourself, you're likely to spend some money on it. Money is just a material manifestation of energy anyway—how are you investing your energy in your well-being? This might be difficult for you at first, especially if you are coming to terms with how your self-worth hasn't been a top priority for you. If you're having trouble justifying the cost of investing in yourself for the support you desire, it may be helpful to tune into this truth: if you want something you've never had, you have to do something you've never done.

And I know perhaps better than anyone that the quickest way to healing self-worthiness and any semblance of a scarcity mentality is to invest powerfully in your transformation by receiving the support you need in embodying your next-level alignment. You're already investing your energetic resources on so many things in your life right now—are you aware of how much abundance you have access to and how you're choosing to channel and allocate it? What would it be like to invest more energy intentionally into healing, transformation, expansion, and growth?

I remember at the time feeling immensely challenged at the prospect of investing a few hundred dollars a month in myself, to pay for someone to support me in this way. (The benefits of this kind of coaching were obvious and I had already felt immediate results from an initial session together, so that helped alleviate my fears.)

Intuition is really a sudden immersion of the
soul into the universal current of life.
—Paulo Coelho, *The Alchemist*

There was really nothing to doubt. But at the time it was hard to invest in myself, especially because I had never done so in this way before.

I mean, really, if you think about *any* way that you spend money, on anything at all—it is an investment. Before, I was investing in alcohol, clothes, and partying. I was indeed spending money on myself, but I wasn't seeing those expenditures in the same light as an investment in coaching because I wasn't choosing to see things that way. I needed a reframe. Investing intentionally in myself (to receive incredible support) was precisely the first step required for me to reframe so many of the false perceptions I had been carrying that ultimately stood in the way of me fully nurturing and embracing my empathic, intuitive gifts while truly owning my power. The investment I made was actually priceless when I thought about the ultimate returns, and later on it would become clear that the more I am willing to invest in myself to support my growth, expansion, and healing, the greater my returns become again and again. Investing in myself to have the support I truly desired was a huge healing step in recuperating my self-worth as well. Every time I invested in myself, I was aligning to a deeper knowing I had within me that I deserved to have my own space to be accountable, witnessed, and supported through everything I desired moving forward. What a loving gift to give yourself, indeed.

WTF IS A LIFE COACH, ANYWAY?

I think we can all agree that you've heard the term *life coach* before. The industry of coaching in general has blown up over the last few years and it can even feel like everyone and their mom is a life coach, offering some kind of service and possibly touting the opportunity to "join a team," perhaps even peddling essential oils or smoothie mixes. I say all of that with the utmost love and appreciation for how the new entrepreneurial economy is evolving…but also with a healthy sense of humor that I know for me continues to be the best medicine. But, I care deeply about life coaching, mentoring, intuitive guidance, and other healing modalities that I've mentioned—I wouldn't be where I am without them.

While there are innumerable definitions of what a life coach is, I'll share with you my own experience and outlook, which is no substitute for your own experience and intuitive guidance. In my heart of hearts, my vision for coaching entails one of a truly sacred nature in which a coach is essentially a holistic, intuitive, strategic guide on assignment to support beings in reconnecting to their own soul-truth; to live life beyond their wildest dreams; to achieve their goals; to grow and heal and transform in all the ways they deeply desire; and to be held accountable to living powerfully, honestly, and most of all, in the utmost freedom and ease.

What's possible to achieve in your work with a coach? It's only determined by how willing you are to go all in and face the truth about yourself, become your own best guide, really allow yourself to access your intuitive guidance, and then act accordingly. In short: your results are dependent on *you*. In fact, a common misconception of coaches is that they'll fix something about you—as though there's something that needs to be fixed. No, not true. A masterful coach knows you are whole and complete already and simply helps mirror this fact back to you so you can feel confident in deciphering your own best guidance and answers to the questions presented to you along your path of embodying your highest alignment. A masterful coach holds you in a safe, secure space in which you know you are loved and free to fully express yourself so whatever is in your way of being your most authentic, powerful self can be naturally processed and released. A masterful coach guides you back to remembrance of your natural state of being, which is optimal wellness, vitality, and vibrancy.

A masterful coach is nothing like a therapist. A masterful coach helps you decipher what actions you can take to best align to your goals and high vision for your life. A masterful coach guides you back to your heart and body connection so you can hear your soul, which contains the ultimate map to your divine destiny. A masterful coach is a stand-in for the truth, and nothing but the truth, and holds you in an energetic field of pure possibility so you are constantly challenged to stretch beyond your comfort zone to grow into new dimensions of power and creativity. A masterful coach reminds you of your infinite potential, your inherent divinity, and your birthright—which is to experience pure love, abundance, thriving vitality, and joyous pleasure.

FINDING A COACH

There are all sorts of coaches out there—you can find one for practically anything these days. What matters most, of course, is to trust your intuition to guide you to whomever you feel can best support you at the time you need it. I find it helpful to consider the following when deciding to work with someone new (the same criteria holds true for clients

I work with as well, actually, because as you know, energy is always a two-way, cocreated street!). Ask yourself these types of questions:

- Is the coach living in integrity?
- Do I resonate with the coach's vision and the way it's communicated?
- Do I trust the coach?
- Do I understand the coach's mode of communication? Am I able to really hear her and receive her deeply?
- Do I believe the coach can help me see myself in the ways I am seeking to be seen?
- Am I willing to go all in with our work together?
- Will I go to any lengths to create the results I truly desire?

Always trust your instincts. You likely gravitate to certain people for a reason—just like clients don't find me by mistake. I see the client-coach relationship as a truly divine connection in which we are being guided toward each other in the most perfect moments because we each have special gifts to share at particular times. Our paths are sometimes meant to cross for a few weeks, a few months, a year, or maybe even lifetimes. How beautiful that we are included in such a divine flow if we are committed to embodying our higher consciousness as vehicles of love and service.

STEPHANIE'S EMPATH EXPERIENCE

The year before I started working with my first coach, I had gone through a tumultuous period in which I felt out of control. My emotional and energetic sensitivity was operating at an all-time high, like a new level of sensitivity had been activated within me. I turned to old habits to numb my intense feelings, overeating in particular, while also taking a break from my movement practices. I started to feel isolated from others, like no one could understand what I was really going through, even when I tried to explain.

During this pivotal, challenging moment, the best thing I could have done was to ask for help and support. I needed someone I trusted to listen to me and provide me with guidance and an open space to simply share my heart. All I really desired was to feel safe and supported, exactly as I was. I was so grateful to connect with a coach who could share her experience and convey the truth that while the journey of an empath might at times feel incredibly lonely, we are never alone.

In fact, quite to the contrary, we are connected not only to each other but to all living beings on the entire planet. And most times, when you're feeling lonely or like the weight of the world is particularly heavy, the best thing you can do to help yourself is ask for help, share your truth, and allow yourself to be supported by someone who you trust understands where you are coming from.

WORKSHOPS AND RETREATS

As soon as you get plugged into your soul community and tribe you'll likely start receiving invitations to participate in immersions, workshops, and other retreat experiences. In fact, consciously seeking out events and immersions that really resonate with you is actually an incredible strategy for finding your tribe that may exist across the globe through many different countries, cultures, and further. Start from where you are and ask what kind of support you are seeking. What kind of growth do you want to experience? What kind of immersive experience feels more enjoyable for you to receive the kind of upgrade or healing you're looking for?

If you aren't already receiving invitations from within your community or your coach, you can most certainly look for events that may speak to you simply by researching online. Social media is a great tool to this end. Are there any authors, spiritual teachers, guides, influencers, or mentors you follow that you really resonate with? See what they're up to as far as hosting retreats and immersive events. If they have a following, chances are they're offering live experiences as a part of their platform. That's a great starting point to see what kinds of immersions you might have easy access to.

I've definitely experienced incredible healing and transformation in group workshop settings and transformational retreats. The more I grew and expanded within my consciousness, the more I found myself craving new types of support systems and communities within which I could be nurtured even more deeply. In addition to twelve-step recovery, I attended various workshops about meditation, yoga, energy healing, art, entrepreneurship, and intuition.

And now I host my own retreats and cohost others around the world, offering tools of transformation, healing, and empowerment. I love the powerful transformation that's possible when groups of visionary souls get together to activate and support one another in healing whatever is preventing each of us from being our best self. Facilitating transformational experiences for groups is one of my favorite things to do ever, and it is absolutely in alignment with my highest excitement—the expression of my own soul's gifts. A friend of mine in Los Angeles runs an immersive workshop called the Magic of Human Connection—the title of which pretty much sums up my vision of retreat experiences. When we gather together to support one another in a common aim, anything is possible. We are all designed to remind one another of our individual and collective magic. And our intimate human connection is the best medicine.

DECIDE WHAT'S RIGHT FOR YOU

As with your entire life, the best way to figure out what kind of support you should use is to look inward. What kind of supportive communities excite you? What feels nourishing? You are invited to experience the magic of self-investment—in mentorship, training, education, coaching, and guidance. On this new path, there's only more growth, and it's limitless. How far do you want to go, how deep, how fast? It's up to you. When you invest in yourself to take big actions and to be accountable to huge vision, you make giant leaps toward bringing to life the dreams you've always had in real, and sometimes surprisingly impressive, ways.

In fact, along the way and as you continue to deepen your understanding of your intuitive, empathic gifts, you might find that you are called to studying healing modalities, health and wellness, or some other kind of continued education. Explore and get creative—see what lights you up! Listen to your intuition, and absolutely trust that it knows the perfect path for you to follow in service to your soul's highest calling.

You have such a special and unique set of gifts to share and you are the only person on the planet who can express them. It's up to you to start digging in to discover what your gifts are so you can share them and experience how healing and expansive it feels to show up as authentically and powerfully as only your soul can.

STAYING GROUNDED AS YOU EVOLVE

You've been empowered with so many new tools and practices to accelerate your healing and incredible evolution into your fullest expression and authentic power. What a beautiful life you've said yes to living! As such you're courageously accepting an immense invitation to do deep transformational work to continue to evolve into a clear channel to allow your gifts to shine through. Celebrate yourself and honor your willingness to show up in more truth—you are so brave. Trust that a beautiful way to celebrate yourself and commit to nurturing your expansive soul going forward is to establish clear practices for staying grounded throughout your imminent evolution.

You've no doubt heard the expression "stay grounded," but what does it actually mean? Being grounded means that you are:

- Present and focused on your physical reality in the moment as opposed to in your head, or daydreaming about something else in the past or future.
- In your body, fully present to the experience that's unfolding in the current moment.
- Stable in your own energy and consciousness.
- Connected to your intuition when you are grounded in your being.
- Able to receive intuitive insights and focus in on what your senses may be guiding you toward.

The skill of being grounded is a top one for empaths to cultivate.

Like many other empaths, I spent the majority of my life experiencing my day-to-day life as extremely ungrounded, which for me manifested as constantly living in my mind, worrying about the past or future, and berating myself over regrets and other dramas I had self-propelled. On top of that, I was subconsciously always trying to avoid being in my body because my sensory experience was too overwhelming, so I purposely avoided sitting still or consciously connecting to my present experience. As I started to awaken to my gifts, I learned not only how important it was to ground myself in my present being but also how nurturing it felt to bring myself back to my stable, centered experience.

And as I continue on a rapidly evolving trajectory of incredible transformation and spiritual expansion, the need to stay grounded in my present experience becomes even more pressing. As the stakes get bigger, as my impact feels more powerful, as my capacity to feel everything that's happening gets amplified, as my intuition gets even more activated, I am reminded now more than ever how important it is to consciously strengthen my ability to be centered and grounded in this moment.

TIPS FOR STAYING GROUNDED

Here are some tools that many empaths find helpful as they practice grounding. I recommend trying them all out, seeing what works for you, and creating your own rituals and practices that you find most nurturing. These tools are meant to be fun and supportive. If anything ever feels like a drag, chances are you're being invited to recalibrate your practice with something that is more in alignment with what your soul truly desires.

- FREQUENT MEDITATION: Of all the things I can suggest when it comes to grounding, having a consistent meditation practice is the most important. How are you starting your morning? Do you wake up in your body or in your mind? Meditate to get into your body, and create space from whatever your mind may be directing you toward. There is a deeper intuitive wisdom trying to be heard. Can you listen?

- INTEGRATION: If you've been experiencing major shifts, sensitivity to shifts in the collective consciousness, undergoing intense transformation and healing—you name it—ensure you are giving yourself plenty of time for integration. Oftentimes going through a major change can inspire incredible excitement and the urge to jump into the next experience immediately, for more healing, more growth, more achievements—the next high. Integration requires taking time to slow down, rest, rejuvenate, and allow your massive transformation to fully land in your being. Allow the fruits of your labor to take their full shape before flying right into the next activating, soul-expanding experience. Healing can become an addiction to some extent in and of itself—whereas integration and patiently allowing your growth and evolution to take its natural course can feel less exciting and at times painfully slow. All of this is a lesson in trust—can you trust the divine flow in which you are absolutely being guided to experience the best life meant just for you? Make sure you are listening to what your body really needs, which may be a prescription for slowing down, resting, nourishing, and not doing much of anything at all.

- CORD OF LIGHT VISUALIZATION: This is a beautiful practice for grounding (which can also count as your meditation ritual). For as long as you need—either a minute or an hour, letting your imagination guide you—visualize a cord of light descending from source energy, the sun, or whatever other higher guidance you believe in, running through your crown chakra at the top of your head all the way through your body, through your feet, into the earth, all the way to the earth's core. Experiment with this visualization and make it your own. However feels best to you is the right way. Try putting on some music as you dive deeper, connecting to higher realms while feeling what it feels like to be fully integrated in your earthly experience all at once.

- DAILY RITUALS: In addition to all the previously mentioned practices, do you have sacred rituals that remind you to ground throughout your day? I've found it fun and immensely supportive to carry crystals in my pockets, in my bag, or around my neck that help me connect to particular energies I feel resonant with. Every time I feel the crystal, I am reminded to connect with the specific intention I set for working with it. Another ritual is to make tea during the day, say a prayer, and set an intention for being grounded in your present-moment experience, releasing anything that is not in service of your highest well-being. It's also very grounding to have intimate conversations with loved ones throughout your day infused with deep listening and authentic relating.

- EATING ROOTS AND EARTHY FOODS: How you nourish yourself is critical to feeling grounded. Consuming stimulants such as sugar, caffeine, and other processed foods can have a disastrous effect on an empath's energy, throwing the body's natural balance incredibly out of whack. Eating root vegetables and other fresh foods from the earth is immensely grounding and supportive for optimal well-being at the cellular level.

- ALL THE FEELS: Are you being hugged and touched in a loving way as much as you truly desire? Nothing is more grounding than tuning into the present-moment experience of sharing an eye gaze, a heart-to-heart hug, or better yet, intensive cuddling in a loving, supportive, cozy space. Have you heard of the hug threshold? According to psychotherapist Virginia Satir, "We need 4 hugs a day for survival. We need 8 hugs a day for maintenance. We need 12 hugs a day for growth." Make sure you're getting your daily dose of love vitamins.

Life is happening now, not yesterday or tomorrow. It may seem overly simple to say, but how often do you forget to truly drop into the now? As you cultivate greater awareness to the present moment, you will see how conditioned you've likely become to be in your mind, which mostly operates only in the past or present. Remember that the only moment in which you can truly ever connect with your highest self, intuition, and soul—which know neither time nor space—is right now, in the body, in its most centered, open, receptive state. Getting grounded is the gateway.

SHARING YOUR GIFTS WITH OTHERS

You are multitalented. And you likely have a knack for knowing what turns others on and lights them up—you have an innate ability to read the collective energy. How do you turn your talents into gifts you can share with the world?

If you've learned anything by now I would hope that you're clear on the fact that your purpose in life is threefold: to enjoy your life immensely; to live in alignment with an incredible flow of infinite abundance, love, and pleasure that's always available to you; and most of all, to carry out your unique soul mission, an assignment that's meant just for you—and only you—to deliver. Your job is to listen and receive fully the invitation that's being presented to you.

If you're now more clear on what your gifts are and how you express them in your highest truth, perhaps you're feeling like your current livelihood isn't completely in alignment with your most authentic self. I've been there, trust me. I know exactly how you feel. It might even be

EXERCISE: EMOTIONAL INTELLIGENCE TECHNIQUES

These techniques are all about becoming completely conscious of your own emotional experience, particularly in relationship to people you find yourself interacting with regularly. They will help you stay grounded and remember that you're the most important person in your life. Here are some key practices to integrate into your daily life to strengthen your ability to read your own energy and emotions as you live your truth.

1. **TO-BE LIST:** Forget about your to-do list; it's time to create something new, all your own. It's a way to fully hold yourself to embodying the powerhouse visionary that you are. A huge part of tuning into your emotional and intuitive guidance is to focus more of your energy on simply being and allowing yourself to embody your most ideal self. How do you desire to BE? Let go of defining yourself at all by what you do, how you help others, what anyone thinks. This is your life after all. How do you want to FEEL? Make a list of the qualities and ways of being that you most desire embodying in your life. Aim for ten, but twenty is even better. After you have your to-be list, imagine some ways that you can support yourself in embodying precisely your desired states. What activities, actions, goals, or tools can you employ in your life to bring those states of being into reality? This commitment is so healing on multiple levels for your emotional state because you are activating incredible self-love and in doing so you are powering up your intuition and soul-centered guidance even more strongly.

2. **KNOW YOUR VALUES:** What do you stand for? What do you believe in? Do you have a core set of values that you live by? If you know what you stand for, it's much easier to stand your ground, maintain your center, and remain uninfluenced by other

people around you either subconsciously or consciously. Create a vision statement for your life. Why are you here? What are you committed to creating? What is your mission? Own it, spend time with it every day, and meditate on your values to ensure they are kept up to date to accurately reflect your highest truth. When you know who you are, why you are here, and what you truly stand for no matter what, you become less susceptible to codependency, energetic drains in relationships, and other avenues of negativity or toxicity.

3. **EMOTIONAL AWARENESS:** Try tracking the emotional states that come up throughout the day for a week or so and notice if you see any patterns between certain times of the day, recurring situations you find yourself in, or certain people you are interacting with. You can keep a simple list by noting the time frame (perhaps setting a timer to check in each hour), and writing your emotional experience as well as anything else you observe being present for you. Once you have your daily and weekly data, what do you notice? Any patterns? What's the proportion of negative to positive experiences? Any correlations between circumstances? Become a curious inquirer into your emotional state. What an adventure to explore! Prepare to receive some powerful insights into how you can take care of yourself and support yourself even better in feeling how you truly want to feel.

4. **EVERYTHING IS A GIFT:** Here's a challenging exercise, but when practiced with commitment and consistency it's life-changing on so many levels. Whenever you are stressed out, worried, or something bad happens, whenever a challenge arises, whenever you have a negative experience and even when a small part of you is being illuminated perhaps rather painfully, ask yourself: how is this situation the perfect catalyst for my deeply desired next-level

transformation? How is this a gift? Of course, allow yourself to feel the sadness, pain, negativity, anger—and whatever else wants to come up and out—knowing that whatever it is simply wants to be released. But come back to the ultimate question: how is this a gift?

All of these exercises empower you to choose your story and your most ideal, authentic, soul-aligned response. Remember, life is happening *for* you, not *to* you. You have the power to reframe your reality and create a new experience that supports you.

that you're feeling fine where you are—but fine won't cut it any longer because you're no longer willing to settle for less than you deserve. You are ready to go all the way in to full embodiment of your gifts in your most powerful expression and you want to leap into a whole new chapter of life that truly avails you to experiencing it in the ways you've always imagined. It's time. You've done so much incredible work, you've grown so much, and you've transcended huge obstacles. Are you ready to fly?

Before you get settled on jumping ship from your current situation, if that's what in fact feels present for you to do, make sure you're taking care of yourself practically as well as emotionally, energetically, and spiritually. It could also be a ripe opportunity to tune into integration and patience in which you really ascertain where you stand and if where you are does in fact require a drastic transition or overhaul, or if you can instead create slight shifts that may have hugely impactful results. A great way to get grounded in your present reality so you can make a clear decision about where to fly to next—if anywhere—is to revisit your unique gifts. What do you truly have to offer? What within you wants to be expressed? Do you have keys to unlocking your unique soul mission that's waiting to be fully ignited?

UNIQUE EMPATH GIFTS

Here are some other examples of empath superpowers that you may very well identify within yourself (or within other empaths you're close to):

- CROSS-CULTURAL COMMUNICATION: The ability to write and speak in a tone and style that resonates with a wide array of people.
- MEDIATION, NEGOTIATION, AND CONFLICT RESOLUTION: An uncanny ability to be an unbiased third party that helps facilitate clarifying discourse, particularly in intense or chaotic situations.
- FACILITATION OF TRANSFORMATION, GROWTH, AND HEAL-ING: A powerful ability to hold space for the transformation of

others, indicative of the space that's been created through the empath's own commitment to self-healing and growth.

- ACTIVE LISTENING: A notable ability to listen deeply to others while patiently and accurately understanding what inspires their particular intentions and behaviors.
- EXPERT MARKETERS: A keen ability to understand how to position products and messages with powerful magnetism by tuning into what the collective really desires.
- TREND-SETTING AND FORECASTING: A seemingly effortless capacity to tell what direction the market is going in, what will be a new trend, and what will be on the way out (as such, positions involving investing, development, strategy, and marketing are well-aligned to someone who is empowered in their empathic abilities).

MEGHAN'S EMPATH EXPERIENCE

Prior to my awakening, the biggest challenges I faced on a daily basis were fear of success and fear of the unknown. These beliefs kept me in a holding pattern, keeping me stuck without any change. I was freezing and in a constant state of inaction.

Then I attended a powerful retreat focused on healing my inner child and immediately afterward I experienced the most magical results. I felt like my authentic self, unafraid to share who I was. I felt newly empowered to take aligned steps into the direction of my actual dreams. It felt so good to give myself that gift. I felt liberated.

At the retreat we did an exercise on sharing out loud "what my negative self-talk tells me," which was huge for me because I am so hard on myself in general. As I was saying things out loud to my partner (that I usually said silently to myself), I was sobbing; I was very emotional. It almost felt like someone else was saying them to me. It made me so sad. How dare I let myself talk to myself that way—I didn't deserve it. In terms of my self-worth, I healed this part of myself in a hugely powerful way.

I now exist in a new paradigm based on how my gifts can heal and help others. I am living proof that a naturally insecure person who is so hard on herself and dependent on everyone's approval can grow into an independent, powerful, inspired visionary. Now I am free to detach from the results because I am free of expectations and a need for approval and validation. My entire outlook has shifted.

YOUR GIFTS MAY BE ROOTED IN CHILDHOOD PASSIONS

You might find that some of your adult superpowers were actually evident in your childhood. My earliest memories of what I aspired to be "when I grew up" included a clear vision of becoming president of the United States. I genuinely felt for quite some time that it was through that position that I'd surely be able to make the impact I was here to make and be of utmost service to the collective. That trajectory guided my interests in activism at a young age as well as my pursuit of academic study focusing on political economy, educational equality, social movements, and philosophy.

I remember joining my first activist campaign to save a neighborhood theater near my house in San Francisco from being developed into condominiums when I was around eleven years old. I petitioned my neighbors to fight the construction that would tear down the historic theater, destroying an iconic legacy landmark of San Francisco. I loved the feeling of being part of something bigger than myself and my fourth-grade world. I loved working with other like-minded people, my neighbors in this case, who were similarly dedicated.

That early experience as well as later demonstrations, activist causes, and even being a street canvasser for a political campaign going on at the time (a big one happening in 2008) were all unique expressions of my empathic superpowers being put to use in ways that felt immensely fulfilling. In hindsight, I resonated so deeply with social justice throughout so many of my academic and career motivations because I possessed an innate understanding of world systems even before I could truly fathom the structure of the macro and micro elements entailed; I could feel it all so clearly. This allowed me to utilize my empathy as such a crucial strength in all of my pursuits moving forward and of course throughout my life today.

My experience working in New York City advertising and marketing agencies wasn't such a far cry from my social justice roots either. In fact, in marketing I found such a beautiful alignment with respect to penetrating the collective consciousness.

And as we let our own light shine, we unconsciously give other people permission to do the same. As we are liberated from our own fear, our presence automatically liberates others.
—Marianne Williamson, *A Return to Love*

If you identify with the call to create something new, to embody your truly visionary sole purpose, how do you take the leap? Well, this is certainly a fun game to play that requires all of your empowered strengths to be fully activated: trust, worthiness, and a deep knowing that you are taken care of no matter what, especially the more you seek to align your life to your higher purpose. Simply put, if you are following your best feelings and investing your time and energy into only things that light you up and magnify your ability to give and receive love, you are on the right path. But you may be wondering how that factors into the world in which you may currently find yourself, perhaps in a job that feels more like a dream that you're just now waking up from only to find that your experience of reality isn't so dreamy after all. You have been settling. You haven't been allowing yourself to shine at full capacity. But you're ready now to step up and out from the shadows, and fully into your light. It's time.

Again, you might not want to drop everything and go join a monastery, move to Bali, or create a start-up immediately—although all of these options are absolutely perfect if they're in fact your dream! I however always recommend that you take your time. There's no rush, and like I mentioned, you may find that after taking some time to consider your current situation a bit more clearly that just a few small tweaks can do the trick as opposed to totally jumping ship. So, ask yourself: how did you come to be where you are right now? What is there to celebrate about your current situation? Can you make a pros and cons list of your current work situation? Which is longer, the positives or the negatives?

Whatever it takes for you to find your freedom, that's what you've lived.
—Byron Katie, *Loving What Is*

If your cons most certainly outweigh your pros—and be honest with every point—then it's time for a change. Create a document detailing your intended date of transition out of your current situation as well as your vision for what you'd like to ideally step into. Once you've crafted a time frame for your departure, you'll surely have some other elements to consider such as the amount of money you'd like to save for your safety net to have on hand, any other jobs or opportunities you'd like to start pursuing, and contacts who you'd like to have on your radar regarding possible collaborations. Create the space and see what naturally comes into your field to inspire you. Always remember that regardless of your livelihood, your number one priority and real job for the rest of your life is to take incredible care of yourself. It's only by continuing to follow the relentless self-care practices that have empowered you so fully in being your best self that you will continue to live your most extraordinary life. Keep following your feel-good principles and practices and trust that more will continue to be revealed.

IT'S TIME TO FLY

Relax. Surrender. Trust. Repeat.

You are being asked to surrender the old.
The old constructs that no longer work.
They never worked, actually, but you needed them to learn what you came here to learn.
You experienced codependency so you could learn independence.
You experienced loneliness and isolation so you could witness true love and intimacy.
You lived in fear and scarcity so you could master abundance and cultivate unshakable trust in the divine.
You abused your power so you could learn what it feels like to live in complete cooperation and harmony, in accordance with natural law.

You are here in this now to complete your lessons.
To master prosperity.
To embody love.
To step into your true power and self-leadership.

There are no victims.
A victim is simply someone who doesn't take initiative.
Initiative is another word for initiation.
Consider this an initiation into your next-level freedom.
Expansion.
Desire.
Truth.

You are being called to RISE.

To trust your heart-led intuition.
And put your ego-driven mind to rest.
Let your heart lead you forward.
Into the most beautiful dance you've ever imagined.

Unplug from the old paradigms that no longer serve.
They're so worn out, you can feel them weighing you down.
They're not even yours.
They belong to the collective, and to so many other souls who have
not yet caught up to you on your path.

Need help unplugging?
Ask.
Or keep trying to figure it out yourself.
Until it gets painful enough to finally surrender.
But know it doesn't have to get worse before it can get better.
It doesn't have to be so hard, or hard at all, actually.

That's why we're here.
We're flying into the new collective experience—can you feel it?
It's all perfectly on time. Meant to be.
It might feel reminiscent of times long since passed.
We are all remembering.

This time you get to set yourself free.

You choose.
No one is here to save you.
Because you don't need saving.
It may feel like you do.

The Empath Experience

Can't someone just give you the answer?
Or the map?

Truth is you have it all and you always have.
And it's YOURs to navigate.
But sometimes it's helpful to have a guide.
A guide to come back to YOU.
And listen.

You see, you've learned to stop listening and stop trusting YOU.
But you are the map holder. The light bearer. The go-to guide.
If you've gone off course it's because you're not trusting you.
Need help plugging back into your TRUTH and TRUST?

That's what I'm here for. In fact, that's precisely why I DO WHAT
I DO.
That's the whole point, actually.
You see, I'm not here to save anyone.
Or be a guru.
Or be put on a pedestal.

You are here to become so awakened to embody the TRUTH that's
available to us all.
To simply be a mirror for everything we are all capable of
experiencing.
So you remember, you have everything you've ever needed and
wanted all along—everything you crave to experience, you can give to
yourself.
Now. You don't even need to wait.

And as you up-level it might feel like everything is crumbling.

It's Time to Fly

It is. So you can build a new foundation at an even higher elevated level than before.

A new normal.

A new baseline.

It will feel shaky and perhaps terrifying.

Like you want to quit and back down.

This is all a test for you to CHOOSE your path yet again.

To confirm with yourself that YOU are the one you are here for.

That you LOVE you no matter what and recommit to showing up fully for whatever it is your HEART is yearning to experience.

You are your own best leader.

You are a cocreator with the infinite.

Are you stepping up to the plate?

Tell me, what are you here for?

What do you believe is possible for YOU?

Remember who you are.

Remember why you came here.

You are infinite.

RESOURCES

BOOKS

Anatomy of the Spirit by Caroline Myss

The Aquarian Empath by Irma Kaye Sawyer

Become the Most Important Person in the Room by Rose Rosetree

The Divine Matrix: Bridging Time, Space, Miracles, and Belief by Gregg Braden

Emotional Freedom by Judith Orloff

The Empath's Survival Guide: Life Strategies for Sensitive People by Judith Orloff

Energetic Boundaries by Cyndi Dale

Energy Medicine by David Feinstein and Donna Eden

The Highly Sensitive Person by Elaine N. Aron, PhD

The Intuitive Dance by Atherton Drenth

Quantum Warrior: The Future of the Mind by John Kehoe

The Surrender Experiment: My Journey Into Life's Perfection by Michael A. Singer

The Untethered Soul: The Journey Beyond Yourself by Michael A. Singer

ARTICLES

- Akashic records: www.edgarcayce.org/the-readings/akashic-records/
- Empath survival guide: www.mindbodygreen.com/0-28157/6-ways-to-deal-when-you-feel-everything-an-empaths-survival-guide.html
- Human energy fields: http://energeticsinstitute.com.au/science-of-human-energy-fields/
- Life as an empath: www.mindbodygreen.com/0-28156/im-an-empath-i-feel-everything-heres-what-its-really-like.html
- Life as an empath: www.huffingtonpost.com/tree-franklyn/youre-not-an-alien-youre-an-empath_b_7763702.html

- Life as an empath: www.vice.com/en_us/article/dp3jva/what-its-like-to-be-an-empath-hsp-psychic-new-age
- Pranayama: www.yogajournal.com/poses/types/pranayama
- Quantum possibilities: www.quantumpossibilities.biz/clairs
- Sound healing: www.mindbodygreen.com/0-17515/what-you-need-to-know-about-sound-healing.html
- ThetaHealing: www.thetahealing.com

MEDITATION RESOURCES

- Against the Stream: www.againstthestream.org
- The Big Quiet: www.bigquiet.nyc
- Deep Mindfulness Collective: www.youtube.com/user/Januszwelin
- Dharma Punx: www.dharmapunx.com
- Inscape: www.inscape.life
- Insight Timer: www.insighttimer.com
- Journey Meditation: www.journeymeditation.com

SPIRITUAL TEACHERS

- Alan Watts: www.alanwatts.com
- Amma: www.amritapuri.org
- Deepak Chopra: www.deepakchopra.com
- Erin-Ashley Kerti: www.youtube.com/user/reverendkerti
- John of God: http://johnofgod.com
- Kaypacha Lescher: http://newparadigmastrology.com
- Marianne Williamson: https://marianne.com
- Matt Kahn and Julie Dittmar: www.truedivinenature.com
- Osho: www.osho.com
- Pema Chödrön: https://pemachodronfoundation.org
- Yogi Bhajan: www.yogibhajan.org

INDEX